THORNY ISSUES

THORNY ISSUES

HOW ETHICS AND MORALITY
AFFECT THE WAY WE LIVE

by John Langone

Little, Brown and Company   Boston   Toronto

12387

FIRST EDITION

Library of Congress Cataloging in Publication Data

Langone, John, 1929–
  Thorny issues.

  Includes bibliographical references.
  Summary: Analyzes our ideas of morality and ethics
and considers social issues such as human rights,
war, and capital punishment and ethics in medicine,
business, journalism, and other fields.
  1. Social ethics — Juvenile literature.
[1. Ethics] I. Title.
HM216.L29   170   81–12318
ISBN 0–316–51430–6   AACR2

BP

Published simultaneously in Canada
by Little, Brown & Company (Canada) Limited

PRINTED IN THE UNITED STATES OF AMERICA

For Gia and Albert

Contents

THORNY ISSUES

Introduction

—•◆•—

Ａges ago, in Greek legend, Hecuba and her husband, Priam, King of Troy, consulted with a soothsayer. This foreteller of events predicted that the couple would have a child, named Paris, and that he would bring about the death of his family, the downfall of his native city, and the ruin of his country.

To prevent such a catastrophe, Hecuba and Priam ordered Paris strangled as soon as he was born. However, the slave who was assigned to carry out the murder left the infant on the top of Mount Ida, where a group of shepherds found and cared for him.

The tale may be used to illustrate a consideration that underlies many debates, dilemmas, and ethical concerns — does the end justify the means? In the case of Paris, his death was ordered to ensure a greater good — the survival of his family, and his nation.

The question of the worth of the individual versus the worth of the many is only one of the perplexing questions that will come up in the following pages. The study of ethical problems revolves around questions — and few, if any, answers. This ambiguity can be most frustrating and irritating in a world that often relies on the courtroom dictum of "Answer the question, yes or no." It is hoped that the questions that arise herein will make you more sensitive to the issues raised, and although the material included won't always tell you how to find answers, it will at least offer you ways to examine the issues, and provide you with some alternatives.

This is not a book about philosophy or personal morality. It will not tell you whether or not to have sex, or to drink, or to go to church or temple, or whether you exist or only think you do. It is, rather, a book about some — but not all, by any means — of the everyday and not-so-everyday dilemmas that are faced by scientists, politicians, business people, journalists, physicians, theologians, and law-enforcement agencies. But though the issues discussed confront, for the most part, professional people, this does not mean that you should be left out of the debates. Apart from helping you to think a bit more on such matters as personal responsibility, justice, and obligation — and helping you to understand the decision-making process — the issues that will be raised do, in some way, touch all our lives. Whether or not to wage war and the manner in which it is waged are questions that affect our daily well-being. Whether a scientist is to be allowed to experiment on human beings, to manipulate genes and create some new, and possibly horrible, life form, affects us. Mercy killing, civil disobedience, draft evasion, abortion, capital punishment, torture, slavery, and the individual's right to privacy versus the public's right to know — all of these are subjects into which ethics intrudes. Each involves social responsibility and personal values. If they are left undiscussed, the conflicts that are at their root will remain submerged, and this silence can only strengthen any misconceptions you might have about them.

Again, definitive answers cannot be given. But if you learn to recognize the ethical issues, and to analyze them, chances are that you'll resolve some of the quandaries — at least to your own satisfaction. Your own values will enter into the decision-making process, and so, too, will those of others. You'll ask yourself, as you consider the situations presented throughout this book, whether you believe in certain rules or absolutes that apply to all — the Ten Commandments, for example, or Natural Law, or the Golden Rule, or the idea that good is the goal of all things, or that the quality of life is always more important than life itself — or whether you believe in shifting your values from situation to situation, applying them to individual circumstances, arguing that what's good today may not be good tomorrow, or what's good for one person may not be good for another. Personal intuition and the belief that human nature has a changeable value, not an absolute one, is the guide of the situation ethicist, who has also been called a "new moralist." Bear in mind, however, that many thinkers have condemned situation ethics as contrary to traditional moral doctrine.

It is not the purpose of this book to change your moral behavior. To attempt that would be to deprive you of the opportunity to "do ethics" — that is, to take a critical look at your values and those of the people around you. Wherever possible, the presentations in the following pages are balanced to present opposing views, and ethical decisions are not deliberately forced upon the reader. The emphasis is on presenting alternatives, and on discussing the consequences of each side's view. The so-called Socratic method — in which the writer tries insofar as is humanly possible to proclaim no truths — is essential if the reader is to think and question.

I rather like the way television commentator David Brinkley once approached this issue of avoiding molds when deciding issues. "I would call myself a liberal," he said in an interview in the *New Yorker* magazine (August 3, 1968), "but not very. I don't like categories. I don't like, for example, the Americans for Democratic Action doctrinaire view of everything that comes along. They look at a problem, decide what the liberal position is, seize it, and then relentlessly defend it. I think that's utter God-damned nonsense. I'm much more pragmatic than that."

Ethics is quite topical these days. Courses are springing up on college campuses, in medical schools, in high schools and junior high schools. The courses are more applied than basic — that is, they relate to such issues as those discussed here: genetics, nuclear power, the law, the difficulties journalists face in presenting information to the public, truth-telling in a hospital setting, and so on.

So no matter what you've thought in the past about this branch of philosophy that asks and attempts to answer questions about what is right and what should be done, bear one essential fact in mind: The subject is more than an exercise for philosophers and theologians. It does relate to our everyday values and activities.

One other thing. You won't come to any conclusions through divine inspiration — at least I don't think so — while reading this book. Rather, be prepared to resolve some of the dilemmas ahead through what Cicero called "the guide and light of life" — reason.

[1]

History of Ethics

IMAGINE that you live in a society with no rules or regulations, where everyone acts just as he or she pleases and purely for their own interests. Carlo Collodi, who wrote *Pinocchio*, created such an environment in his Land of the Boobies, a country in which there was no school on Thursdays, and every week consisted of six Thursdays and one Sunday, where the days were spent in play and amusement, where all was happiness and contentment.

But the boys who chose this seemingly idyllic life paid a price, as you all know. Pinocchio and his fun-loving friends were transformed into donkeys just like those, Collodi wrote, that draw carts and carry cabbages and salads to market.

Such a dramatic result would not occur, of course, if we lived only for ourselves, without rules or moral codes. But things would be bad enough. If you always thought only of yourself, chances are you wouldn't think about being loyal to anyone. You might betray those around you, and be betrayed by them. There would be no reason to distinguish between right and wrong because whatever you felt was right would be right.

Fortunately, such societies do not exist, if only because a society can't exist without individuals caring about one another. Virtually every society has some standard of ethical conduct that prohibits irrational and random violence, and upholds the spirit of the Good Samaritan and the Golden Rule.

"The conditions of a satisfactory human life for people living in groups could hardly obtain otherwise," observes William K. Frankena of the University of Michigan. "The alternatives would seem to be either a state of nature in which all or most of us would be worse off than we are, even if Hobbes is wrong in thinking that life in such a state would be 'solitary, poor, nasty, brutish, and short'; or a leviathan civil state more totalitarian than any yet dreamed of, one in which the laws would cover all aspects of life and every possible deviation by the individual would be closed off by an effective threat of force."[1] (Thomas Hobbes, 1588–1679, was an English philosopher who argued that human beings are motivated only by selfish considerations such as desire for power, and that without an all-powerful ruler, our lives would be grim.)

In some societies, ethics is closely tied to religion; Judaism uses its belief in a just God, who is the model of our striving toward goodness, and in the Ten Commandments, as elements that affect personal and societal morality; Christianity drew heavily on Judaism for its ethical principles; and Muslims and Buddhists are much concerned with human actions in everyday life. Self-sacrifice, mercy, love, justice, prudence, courage, kindliness, and nonviolence are woven in and out of these religions, and each of these qualities plays a role in our decisions in moral matters.

Other philosophies base their ethical precepts on non-religious beliefs. Humanists, for example, stress the importance of the human race and its place in the universe, arguing that men and women are at the center of concern, possess worth and dignity, and therefore deserve to be respected. They believe that the natural and social sciences, not a religion revolving around God's will, are the things that help us make our moral decisions; the emphasis is on the facts of life, not on the mystical elements.

The science of ethics had its origin in ancient Greece, during a time of great political, industrial, and intellectual expansion. All revolved around Athens, a city-state that grew to become the capital of a vast and great empire. Thinkers, dissatisfied and restless, were eager to breathe new life into theories that had focused on abstract concepts such as the nature of reality and the structure of the universe. Right and wrong, justice and injustice — these emerged as the subjects for critical analysis.

The familiar names of the Sophists, Socrates, Plato, and Aristotle are closely linked to the earliest ethical theories. This is not the place to give any detailed account of the intricacies of their thinking, but suffice it to say the following about each:

The Sophists were teachers of rhetoric and political and moral doctrines, who were accused by other philosophers of being more interested in successful argument than in arriving at the truth. Some of them even denied there was such a thing as truth, and argued that morality did not exist except in the minds of the people. It was the will of those in power, said the Sophists, that determined what was right or wrong for everyone.

Socrates was a systematic doubter and questioner who stressed seeking the truth in everyday life, believed that knowledge was the highest virtue, and had as his watchword, "Know thyself."

Plato, Socrates' most famous pupil, stressed the search for happiness and justice, arguing that if one knows what the good and the right are, one will not go wrong. Evil, he said, is bred by lack of knowledge.

Aristotle, pupil of Plato, taught that contemplation brings happiness, and that a moral being must seek the virtues of courage, justice, temperance, and prudence.

There are other names and theories from the distant past that bear mentioning. The Stoics, for example, argued that human beings should learn to ignore external influences, become independent, and thus become good or evil solely by their own efforts. Happiness is found, they believed, by mastering one's passions and emotions. The Epicureans taught that pleasure was the highest good. But unlike the Hedonists, who sought out intense, fleeting pleasures, Epicureans stressed long-lasting pleasures that were mental rather than physical — music appreciation, reading, an untroubled state of mind. Their idea of "good living" referred to "good" in the highest sense of the word, and they emphasized self-control and prudence in daily life.

Moral philosophy did not, of course, stop with the ancient Greeks. The Christian theologians — men like

Saint Augustine and Saint Thomas Aquinas — related
the Greek virtues to their own concept of morality. Later,
many European philosophers expanded on all that had
been formulated before. There was Baruch Spinoza
(1632–1677), a deeply religious Dutchman who believed
strongly in freedom of thought and expression, and in
the idea that a person's greatest happiness could only
come through understanding that he or she was a tiny
part of God. Immanuel Kant (1724–1804), a German,
argued in favor of a stern morality, suggesting that doing
one's duty is far more important than merely seeking
happiness or making others happy. Thus, he said, a gen-
uine moral act is one that is performed purely out of
respect to duty. Other philosophers, like the Scotsman
David Hume (1711–1776) and the Englishman John
Stuart Mill (1806–1873), took a different approach.
Hume taught that only those characteristics that are agree-
able or useful are virtuous, and Mill, the leader of the
utilitarian movement, argued that our moral decisions
should be governed by the need to bring the greatest
happiness to the greatest number of people. And of course
there was Niccolò Machiavelli (1469–1527), the Italian
statesman and student of politics whose name has been
linked down through the years to all that is devious in
political action. Machiavelli put forth the notion that
politics was amoral — outside the range of moral judgments — and that a ruler need not worry about the means
used to achieve a goal; any means, no matter how wicked,
could be employed to deter one's enemies and control
one's subjects.

It should be obvious from all of this that what the

standard of morality ought to be — that is, what we should or should not do — is a matter of many opinions. Some say the standard is God's, others that it is the result of pure reason; still others feel that it is simply what brings us or a group of people pleasure.

Compounding the difficulty is the question of whether we are free to make the choices, or whether they are determined for us. On the one hand, there are those who say we are free to make a reasonable selection from several choices — not necessarily that we will always make the right choice, only that we can choose if we want to, and are able to do so because our minds are unhindered. On the other hand, the determinists believe that people don't really make choices at all, that everything that happens, including our choices, is the result of other events.

We all realize, I'm sure, that there are some things in life over which we have little or no control. We've all given in to strong temptations, doing things we know we shouldn't do. We've all lost our tempers, no matter how hard we tried not to, and we've all broken promises. What is important to know is that sometimes the things we do are determined for us, sometimes they are not — but that there is nothing except time and a mental incapacity of some sort to stop us from at least deliberating what we might do, thinking through the alternatives and the consequences of each act, of each decision.

Dr. Frankena has this to say about that:

> Socrates first lays down some points about the approach to be taken. To begin with, we must not let our decisions be determined by our emotions, but must ex-

amine the question and follow the best reasoning. We must try to get our facts straight and keep our minds clear. Questions like this can and should be settled by reason. Secondly, we cannot answer such questions by appealing to what people generally think. They may be wrong. We must try to find an answer we ourselves regard as correct. We must think for ourselves. Finally, we ought never to do what is morally wrong. The only question we need to answer is whether what is proposed is right or wrong, not what will happen to us, what people will think of us, or how we feel about what has happened.[2]

It's not as easy, of course, as it sounds — especially that part about whether what we do is right or wrong.

How we determine right and wrong is not something that this book, or any other one for that matter, can answer satisfactorily. We might believe that what is good is right, and that what is good is pleasure, or virtue, or knowledge, or justice. We might say that an act is right and ought to be done if it is designed to bring about more good than evil, or is better than another alternative in that respect. Or, we might reject the notion that a choice of good over evil is an infallible rule and say, instead, that each case must be decided individually, that in some circumstances the wrong, or what is perceived as wrong, is the road to be chosen.

We are all human beings, and each of us makes decisions for our own special reasons. Lawrence Kohlberg, professor of education at Harvard University, has identified six stages of moral reasoning that individuals pass through. At stage one, our reasons for acting in moral situations are fear of punishment or anticipation of reward or favor. The physical consequences of action, says Kohlberg, determine its goodness or badness, regardless of the human meaning or value of these consequences.

In stage two, right action consists of those things that satisfy our own needs, and once in a while, the needs of others. There is an element of "You scratch my back and I'll scratch yours" in this stage of development, not of loyalty, gratitude, or justice.

At stage three, we view good behavior as that which pleases or helps others and is approved by them. We conform to stereotypical images of what is majority, or "natural," behavior. In general, we earn approval by being "nice."

When we reach stage four, we lean toward authority, or fixed rules, and the maintenance of social order. Right behavior consists of doing one's duty, showing respect for authority, and maintaining the given social order for its own sake.

At stage five, which is where, Kohlberg says, the men who wrote the U.S. Constitution were, right action is defined in terms of general individual rights, protected by contract, and standards that have been agreed upon by the whole society.

Stage six, as one Harvard student put it, is written with golden chalk. At this lofty point, the universal principles of justice and equality of human rights, and respect for the dignity of human beings as individuals, dominate, and rise above rules or social contracts.

Our decisions about what is right or wrong, then, are born of many needs and beliefs. But one cannot ignore that intangible quality known as human feeling. There comes a time in all our lives when the desires and rules that usually govern us do not seem to be working, when we can reason forward and backward on opposite sides of a question without coming up with an answer, when a situation is as clear as it ever will be, when we can have no more facts about a dilemma. It is then that the gift known as intuition, that knowledge we gain without rational thought or inference, comes into play, and we know, sometimes suddenly, what it is we need to know to decide.

[2]

Medical Ethics

———•—•———

Not too many years ago, all a physician was required (and trained) to do was diagnose illness and attempt to treat it with a limited variety of drugs and surgical procedures. For the patient, being sick meant seeking out treatment and placing oneself in the hands of the practitioner. Rarely, if ever, did a patient ask too many questions of the doctors — who were just as happy with that arrangement, since they did not encourage that any be asked.

The doctor was truly in control — in some instances, too much so, as in the apocryphal story of the physician who stood over his patient when she awoke from surgery and told her in words that she would always remember, "Do you see these hands, madam? They saved your life."

Nurses had their role as handmaidens of the physician, pharmacists merely filled the prescriptions the doctors wrote, hospitals admitted, bedded, and billed the patients. Today, all of that has changed. Doctors and nurses still care for the sick, druggists still sell medication, and hospitals still function as they did in the early days. But pharmacists have become health educators, nurses are performing many of the tasks previously assigned only to doctors, and the doctors — backed up by computers and heart-lung machines, incredibly complex whole-body x-ray scanners, and a host of other products of medical high technology — are able to perform near miracles today that probably would have been regarded as pure magic by Hippocrates, the most celebrated and learned physician of antiquity, the "father of medicine."

It is this ability to do so many remarkable new things — transplant hearts and kidneys, replace organs and arteries and bones with factory-made duplicates of plastic and metal, keep the dying alive indefinitely with machinery and artificial blood and wonder medicines — that has forced the physician and all other members of the health-care teams to pay a good deal more attention to the patient, not merely as a "case," but as a person with rights and dignity. With such heightened awareness comes an array of awesome ethical questions that are being aired with increasing frequency in hospitals, medical schools, and courthouses across the country.

Dr. Edwin N. Foreman, who works with young cancer patients at Rhode Island Hospital, has aptly summed up the feelings of those who must face such questions on a daily basis: "I have in my hip pocket the mechanisms for keeping people alive, but I worry about the quality of life. I see families that are distressed and I see patients who are suffering or frightened. I can make the decisions. I can do what I please, what makes me most comfortable emotionally. But I am worried, as I think most physicians are, about what is the 'right' thing to do. In other words, someone is dying and you can put them on a respirator and keep them alive for a year, or you can let them die naturally in a day."[1]

The patients, too, are increasingly aware of the medical dilemmas, many of which have been given extensive media coverage over the past few years. They are demanding to be included in the decision-making process; they do not perceive the doctor as a godlike figure as readily as they did in the past; they have asked that more truth be told them about their conditions.

As Dr. Foreman expresses it, "It isn't just the physicians who have to make these choices. It's often the family and the loved ones who can't let them go. The patient is not completely informed of what's going on, so he doesn't enter into a decision rationally. He sees his panicked family urging some procedure — to have a tracheotomy so he can breathe a little longer, to undergo surgery that can only prolong an agonizing life."[2]

In this chapter, we will examine some of the troubling questions that are being considered by ethicists, physicians, and legal specialists. Some of the situations have been resolved — which does not necessarily mean that the decisions are correct ones; others have not. Remember that in ethics, there is not always one answer — in fact, it has been argued that there are never any answers to fit the definition of the word *answer*, "a correct response." Remember also that the conflict you are attempting to re-solve may be between two goods, not between one good and one evil, as in the classic confrontation that one so often encounters in literature and liturgy; thus, there may be two "right" answers. There may also be several answers, each one acceptable to someone.

Against that background, let's examine some of the key ethical concerns that have emerged in the practice of modern-day medicine — bearing in mind that there are infinitely more than could possibly be presented in a survey of this sort. For our purposes, the discussion will be limited to four broad areas — treatment of the dying patient, truth-telling, deciding who gets scarce and expensive medical treatment, and experimenting on humans.

The Dying Patient

Undoubtedly, you have heard the expression "pulling the plug," which refers to someone in authority in a hospital turning off the machinery that supports the life of a dying patient, or withholding drugs or other essential treatment. Such an act, when it is done to put sufferers or the hopelessly ill out of their misery, is referred to as "mercy killing," or euthanasia (from the Greek words *eu,* meaning "good," and *thanatos,* "death").

Direct euthanasia, which is a deliberate act to end a patient's life — administering a poisoned drink, for instance, or a lethal injection — is not legally permissible in any civilized country. No human being has the right, says the law, to take another's life, unless in self-defense, in a just war, or in executing a condemned criminal. If you take your own life, it is suicide — still considered a grave wrong, if no longer a criminal act — and if some-one does it for you, at your request or not, he or she is guilty of murder.

But acts of passive euthanasia in which a doctor or a nurse does not do the thing that can prolong one's life — by withholding medication, for instance — are not un-usual occurrences. Nor is the situation in which a suffering patient who has lost all hope refuses the treatment that might prolong his or her life.

Euthanasia advocates — and the word *euthanasia* must be used with care since it is a general term that does not take into account the differences between direct, passive, voluntary, and compulsive forms of the practice — be-lieve that incurably ill individuals have the right to have their lives ended gently, whenever and however they choose. Suffering with no hope of cure, they feel, is de-grading and demoralizing, and drains life of its meaning. To euthanasia advocates, life is a qualitative, not a quan-titative, state — that is, it is better to live a life worth living than simply to be alive. The argument is made that refusing to go along with a hopelessly ill patient's request for an end to it all is not only inhuman treatment of the patient, but places an enormous emotional and financial strain on the surviving family members. This last point is a special consideration in light of the high cost of medical care today, and the need of hospitals to keep beds occupied and expensive equipment in use. Shouldn't all this high-priced and high-powered medical expertise be put to better and more productive use, goes the argument, by limiting it to those patients with some chance of recovery and some promise for a meaningful life?

Opponents of euthanasia argue that only God, the creator of life, has complete mastery over who shall live or die, although some among this group will go along with the right of the state, after due process of law, to take the life of a criminal who has committed an offense punishable by death. Many euthanasia opponents, in answer to the argument that to allow a patient to suffer is inhumane, maintain that too often it is the relatives of the sufferer who cannot tolerate the situation and that it is really they who want to be relieved; their motives are not humanitarian, but selfish. Euthanasia opponents also believe that the doctor's duty is to preserve life, and not to take it or hasten its end for any purpose, no matter how noble. Moreover, they say, the physician who employs euthanasia, with or without a patient's consent, could have made a mistake in diagnosis, and the patient may not have been as seriously ill as believed. They argue that to use the term "incurable" is an admission of defeat; that new cures for the incurable may well be discovered; and that a sufferer might beg for death one day and then change his or her mind later.

Opponents raise a number of other questions: To whom would the euthanasia advocates give the right to take a life? Wouldn't a society with a euthanasia law on its books be tempted to do away with more than the incurable — the elderly, the nonproductive, the emotionally disturbed, or the politically dissident?

There is no doubt that euthanasia poses a number of

very difficult problems, especially for the physician who has been trained to heed the Hippocratic oath, which states in no uncertain terms, "To please no one will I prescribe a deadly drug nor give advice which may cause his death." The International Code of Medical Ethics also warns that a physician must always be aware that he or she is charged with preserving human life until death.

Nevertheless, one continues to hear and read of cases of euthanasia in some form, in which physicians administer lethal doses of medication, switch off life-support systems, or cut nutrients in intravenous feedings of prostrate patients. And there are the cases in which individuals take, often violently, the lives of ill or mentally defective relatives. In many instances of direct mercy killing, the judgment of the courts is lenient, even though such acts cannot be justified legally.

But cases involving passive, indirect acts of euthanasia — stopping treatment so that death will come — are another matter, and much of the discussion of mercy killing today centers on these. There are questions to be asked here as well: Is there really any difference between *killing* a patient with a deadly injection and *letting* that patient die? Might not the motive be the same and, thus, the enormity of the act? Who decides? The patient, the doctor, the relatives, the courts? What criteria must be used to make a decision to withhold life support? Is there a difference between prolonging life and prolonging dying?

Even in the days when resuscitative equipment was not as sophisticated as it is today, when there were no plugs to pull, physicians thought about "letting the patient go" as an alternative to direct forms of euthanasia. Permitting a dying patient to die is called *orthothanasia,* a medical term for natural dying, and there are those who argue that disconnecting a respirator that keeps a dying, incurable patient breathing is orthothanasia because it is not really killing someone but merely withholding an artificial support that is forcing a life to go beyond its natural limits.

Despite the seriousness of allowing a dying patient to die, of letting nature take its course when one knows that nature can be held off with medicine and machinery, there seems to be general agreement that withholding measures in order to hasten death is a *fait accompli* in hospitals throughout the world, and that while one has the obligation to preserve or prolong life, there is no obligation to prolong the act of dying with *extraordinary* means.

Some years ago, the American Society of Abdominal Surgeons took a survey of its members in an effort to sample their attitudes toward death and dying. One of the questions asked was, "As a surgeon, do you believe in prolonging a patient's life with all of the expertise at your disposal, or do you feel there are times when you must let the patient go?"

Nearly a thousand doctors replied, with an overwhelming majority stating they did not believe in prolonging a patient's life with heroic measures. The response ran counter to the argument that most surgeons tend to "go all out" with their patients because they feel that death represents failure. Only twenty-six felt as did one surgeon from New York City, who wrote, "I believe in holding on to a patient until the last minute. We have all seen hopeless cases resurrected." Or, as another did, "I always swing for the fences."

More typical were the following:

"When there is nothing to gain, as in terminal cases, skillful neglect is the procedure of choice."

"One does not try heroics on ninety-nine-year-old patients, but does pull out all the stops on children and young adults."

"I do not approve of prolonging useless life beyond limits nature normally imposes, unless the patient or his family insists on this."

"I do not think a patient's life should be prolonged just to prolong life. Heroic measures are simply not rational or humane."

"My reason is simple and selfish. I have no desire to live as a vegetable, and I am sure most reasonable people will agree."

"There are times when conscientious neglect is the best therapy."

The key word in all of this is *extraordinary*. Most physicians and moralists agree that ordinary means — which have been taken to mean treatment that is easily obtained, holds reasonable hope for some benefit, and is not excessively expensive — must always be employed to preserve life. Not so with extraordinary means, which are life-prolonging methods that do not fit the definition of ordinary ones. Extraordinary means, of course, have their place — for example, when using them can reverse a disease process or allow a person to live without continuing to be dependent on them. But the consensus is that they are not always justified. This raises two important considerations: one is the difficulty in distinguishing ordinary from extraordinary treatment, the other is determining when the latter should be used.

Telling the difference between ordinary and extraordinary measures is not easy because what is extraordinary now may not be so in the future. Penicillin, for example, is an antibiotic that was once considered extraordinary treatment. Today, it is used routinely. Kidney transplants and artificial-kidney machines were once rarities, but today they are standard, though costly, treatment.

If the extraordinary can become the ordinary, does a doctor have a right to base his decision on such a principle?

Closely tied to what constitutes extraordinary treatment is the difficult question of when and whether to employ such means. How does one make the decision? Does the age of the patient have to be a factor? Must the financial means of the patient and his or her family be considered? Is the patient's station in life — poet or derelict or mongoloid, eminent scientist or grocery clerk — important? If "reasonable hope for some benefit" is one reason for using a heroic treatment, how does one measure that benefit? In terms of years added to a patient's life? Recovery from disease? But for how long? Benefit to society? Benefit to the individual? To his or her family? From the physician's standpoint, should he or she order that everything possible be done, to avoid the chance of a malpractice suit being filed by relatives who might feel that the doctor mismanaged the case?

These are troubling questions, and yet each one has been asked in deciding just how far to go in caring for a critically ill patient. Some moralists believe that while extraordinary means may be used, a physician is not obliged to use them — even in cases that are nonterminal, or in cases where a disease is medically curable. This notion takes into account that we are all dying, and that life, therefore, precious as it is, has but limited worth and does not have to be extended at enormous cost and effort.

Pope Pius XII, in a 1957 address, distinguished between ordinary and extraordinary means of treatment, advising that it is not necessary to use heroic measures when recovery is no longer possible. Said the pontiff:

> Natural reason and Christian morals say that man . . . has the right and duty in cases of serious illness to take the necessary treatment for the preservation of life and health. This duty that one has toward himself, toward God, toward the human community, and in most cases toward certain determined persons derives from well-ordered charity, from submission to the Creator, from social justice, as well as from devotion toward one's family. But normally, one is held to use only ordinary means — according to circumstances of persons, places, times, and cultures — that is to say, means that do not involve any grave burden for oneself or another. A more strict obligation would be too burdensome for most men and would render the attainment of the higher, more important, good too difficult. Life, health, all temporal activities are in fact subordinated to spiritual ends. On the other hand, one is not forbidden to take more than strictly necessary steps to preserve life and health, as long as he does not fail in some more serious duty.[3]

In a more recent statement on euthanasia, the Roman Catholic Church continued to condemn the killing of an innocent human being — whether a fetus, an incurable or a dying patient — but allowed dying patients, in some circumstances, to refuse extraordinary and burdensome life-support systems. "When death is imminent," said the Declaration on Euthanasia (1980), "in spite of the means used, it is permitted in conscience to make the decision to refuse forms of treatment that would only secure a precarious and burdensome prolongation of life, so long as the normal care due to the sick person in similar cases is not interrupted."

Consideration of the circumstances is, of course, imperative when determining how much medical expertise to employ, and as distasteful as it might be to consider some of the factors — the patient's age, for instance, or the cost of treatment — each must be examined. Every case is unique, reflecting a combination of conditions — the physical condition, resilience, and will to live of the patient, how essential he or she is to the family's well-being or to the workplace, and the skill of the physicians.

Some might argue that there are moral rules, clear and inflexible, that must be applied in *all* cases involving life and death, but such a hard-line approach is difficult to put into practice. The fact is that each and every decision must be made, ultimately, by human beings who must follow their consciences, who generally are aware that times and rules do change, who often act out of emotion, and who believe, for the most part, that there comes a point where further care is meaningless. Circumstances *do* alter cases, and while there are unquestionably moral rules that we all live by, they are bent every day of our lives. Those who argue against adherence to strict moral principles in the care of the dying are not necessarily unfeeling individuals who believe that their patients are nonpersons. Rather, most are deeply committed to the fundamentals of what might be called biblical ethics, one of the most important of which is the avoidance of injury or suffering of another human being. Most of us are aware that life is a precious commodity, and that to take it automatically or on a mere whim or to hasten the coming of death without justification can only contribute to humankind's all too familiar tendency to violence. We each have a right to life.

Occasionally, however, the emphasis that is placed on the phrase "right to life" obscures the fact that the dying person has the right to die, and to die as peacefully as possible. Under certain circumstances, he or she is not *obliged* to live — and that is a good deal different from one's *right* to live.

That right to die may, in any number of cases, outweigh the intentions of the physician who tries to extend life with a heart transplant or a long-drawn-out resuscitative procedure that can result in nothing more than a comatose patient who only breathes. In such a case human dignity is sacrificed and the process of dying becomes a burden that cannot be justified by any rules, medical or moral.

Again, one must be careful about taking life too lightly, or setting up another kind of rule that tells us exactly when a patient should be allowed to die. A case in point concerns a directive from the superintendent of a London hospital a few years ago. Tacked up on a bulletin board, the notice ordered: "The following patients are not to be resuscitated: very elderly, over 65 years old; malignant disease; chronic chest disease, chronic kidney disease." The notice reportedly ordered that patients in the various categories would have a yellow card marked NTBR (not to be resuscitated) in their records. If such a patient's heart stopped, no attempt was to be made to revive him or her by open chest massage or electrical stimulation. Neither of those procedures falls in the category of extraordinary measures, and reaction to the directive, which was hurriedly taken down, was mixed. A spokesman for the Ministry of Health said that no harm was done in the period the order was on the board, and that it was never actually put into effect. The ministry added that all patients should be considered for resuscitation, and not excluded because of age or diagnostic classification alone.

A spokesman for the British Medical Association said his group could not possibly approve of any such rule. He added that a decision would have to be made by the individual doctor "according to the individual circumstances of the case and not according to any blanket rule."

Circumstances: those changing factors to which we must adapt, cutting our coat, as the saying goes, according to our cloth. Consider the case of a senile, ninety-year-old man dying of a brain tumor. Under normal conditions with a younger patient, the chances of a successful operation are fairly good. This patient, however, is not only elderly but has a heart condition that makes him a poor risk for surgery. It is also discovered that he has developed, while in the hospital, a severe infection that can be treated by administering antibiotics over a long period.

Is anything worthwhile to be gained by operating on this man? Chances are, no. The physicians would undoubtedly agree that the operation, ordinary under other circumstances, would be extraordinary in this case. Moreover, they might not even want to use ordinary means to fight his infection, given the patient's chances of surviving his terminal illness for any length of time. So a decision is made — by the man's wife and children, since his mental faculties have been lost — to do nothing but make him comfortable, and let death come quietly when it will come.

As stated, this particular case is not especially difficult to resolve, and the decision to let the patient die would be considered a wise judgment. But there are all sorts of circumstances that might make one think a bit more before jumping to a conclusion.

What if the man had no heart condition, and was not a poor surgical risk? Would the operation be worth trying then? Would the fact that he was senile enter into the judgment? What if he were senile, but only fifty years old? Would the operation be justified? What if he were not senile, and could make the decision himself? Should his wishes — to be operated on despite the risks, or left to die — be honored? What if, senile, he had no relatives, no friends, and was a ward of the state? Who, then, would make the decision?

That last question is probably the most important and difficult one in medical ethics. Ideally, of course, the patient would make the decision, and whether or not he opted for the surgery, his physician probably would accede to his request.

Some people put their wishes in writing before they become ill. In 1976, California passed the Natural Death Act, the first law enacted in the nation to recognize an individual's right to request that his or her life not be prolonged by artificial means when death is believed imminent. The so-called Living Will provides that the signer's condition be certified as terminal by two physicians, and states: "When the application of life-sustaining procedures would serve only to artificially prolong the moment of my death, and where my physician determines that my death is imminent whether or not life-sustaining procedures are utilized, I direct that such procedures be withheld or withdrawn and that I be permitted to die naturally."

There is also a clause stating that if the patient is unable to express his or her desires as death nears, the document is to be honored by family and physicians as "the final expression of the legal right to refuse medical or surgical treatment and accept the consequences of such refusal."

The lawmaker who introduced the bill, Assemblyman Barry Keene, said he felt that the legislation was the result of a generation's "searching for ways to rehumanize the dying process, and the product of a generation which views with horror the confrontation between modern technology and the human needs of dying."[4]

In the past few years, a number of states have followed California's lead and enacted right-to-die laws — among them Washington, Kansas, Arkansas, Idaho, Nevada, New Mexico, North Carolina, Oregon, and Texas. Bills have been considered by many other states, a trend hailed by the New York–based Society for the Right to Die as one aimed at changing the plight of dying patients who are being kept alive by medical technology "far beyond the point where real life ends."

Opponents of such legislation — some religious groups, lawyers, and physicians — argue that living wills actually legalize mercy killing and suicide, that they encroach on a doctor's responsibility and judgment, or that they could be misused by greedy or unfeeling heirs who would bene-fit if a relative near death could be persuaded to sign.

But not every patient (or potential patient) will sign a living will, or be able to communicate his or her desires. The senile, the retarded, and patients in a coma are not capable of making decisions, and in these cases it is usu-ally the family and the doctors who, after consultation, decide not to operate, or to withhold medication, or even to administer a drug ostensibly for pain or sedation but that is also known to hasten death under the circum-stances. Sometimes the family does not feel qualified to make a judgment, or the members are unwilling to take on such an enormous responsibility. They ask the doctors what is best, and then simply go along with that advice.

Most of this agonizing and counseling and ultimate action goes on behind closed doors, and generally no one but the family and physicians are involved. But some of these cases become public knowledge because of their uniqueness, their complexity, or simply because someone has decided that the issues involved are ones the public should be aware of.

The Karen Ann Quinlan case is one that has drawn the public into the sensitive discussion of who should decide to treat or not to treat those incapable of making such a decision for themselves. In addition, the Quinlan case, and others like it, has focused on the role of the courts in determining if life support may be cut off or withheld.

In the spring of 1975, Karen Ann, twenty-one years old, was rushed to St. Clare's Hospital in Denville, New Jersey, in a near-death coma. She had suffered permanent and irreversible brain damage, apparently caused when she took a combination of alcohol, tranquilizers, barbiturates, aspirin, and quinine. Kept alive with an artificial breathing device, and fed intravenously, the young woman lay in an intensive-care unit of the hospital in a state of profound unconsciousness from which she could not be aroused, even by the most powerful stimuli.

Karen Ann's parents, acting in agreement with their parish priest, asked that the physicians turn off the respirator and allow her to die. The doctors refused, claiming that to do so would violate their concept of medical ethics, and so, too, did the hospital. The patient's parents then petitioned the state superior court for the right, as parents, to turn off the machine that kept Karen Ann alive. Again, the request was denied.

The case was finally appealed to the New Jersey Supreme Court, which reversed the decision of the lower court, and ruled that the respirator could be disconnected if everyone agreed that Karen Ann, who had shriveled to eighty pounds, would not emerge from her coma and that her brain damage was irreparable. The high court also found that Karen Ann had the right to refuse medical treatment, and that the right to express that wish could be transferred to her guardian, in this case, her father. The court concluded, moreover, that the medical profession's standards of ethics are, in some degree, protective of the physician who is concerned over legal liability. Furthermore, it said that a hospital ethics committee could be brought into future cases to review the decision of doctors, guardian, and family, and thus decide on a course of action without involving the courts. Said Karen Ann's father after the ordeal: "Right along, this decision seemed so natural. Everything was natural all the way along. . . . Because we were told by all the doctors the case was hopeless, it just naturally followed that we should turn off the machine and put her back in her natural state. Could we have made the decision if we weren't religious? I know that religion was a great source of strength and comfort. What I meant was that it just naturally followed that there was nothing else we could do."[5]

At this writing, the Karen Ann Quinlan case has not been fully resolved, for the young woman, freed of machines and monitors, still lives, awaiting a natural death. Her controversial story is now private, but the issues raised are public ones. Does the fact that the young woman was still alive even after the life-support systems were shut down make any difference? Did the court's involvement set a dangerous precedent by taking decision-making away from physicians who felt that their medical ethics would be violated if they turned off the machinery? Does the appointment of an ethics committee suggest a "God Squad" approach — that is, decision-making by a supposedly infallible body?

Says George Annas, director of the Center for Law and

Health Sciences, Boston University School of Law, of the court's involvement in whether to continue or withhold life-sustaining treatment from patients unable to make the decision themselves: "Judges are asked to decide this question, not because they have any special expertise, but because only they can provide the physicians with civil and criminal immunity for their actions. In seeking immunity, legal considerations quickly transcend ethical and medical judgments."[6]

Although the Quinlan case is the best known of its genre, there are others that merit our consideration. One of these is the case of Joseph Saikewicz, a sixty-seven-year-old retarded ward of the state of Massachusetts at the Belchertown State School. Saikewicz, who had been a resident of the school for forty-eight years, had a mental age equivalent to that of a three-year-old child, and was diagnosed, in 1976, as suffering from an acute and usually incurable form of leukemia.

Doctors testified that in his case, the use of drugs would result in survival for a few months but would, however, cause serious painful side effects. The physicians said also that because Saikewicz would not understand the reason for his pain, he would probably have to be physically restrained during the weeks the drugs were administered.

With this information, the superintendent at the institution petitioned the Hampshire County Probate Court to appoint a guardian empowered to make a decision regarding treatment. Together with two physicians, the guardian advised against treating the man. Subsequently, Judge Harry Jekanowski ruled that it would not be in the patient's best interests to be given the chemotherapy, and he immediately submitted the case to the Massachusetts Supreme Court — which affirmed the probate court's ruling.

Where the Quinlan court had entrusted the young woman's fate to a guardian and suggested that future cases could be resolved by an ethics committee without resort to the courts, the Massachusetts Supreme Court's ruling implied that such matters are the province of the probate courts. (A probate court is one established to administer the estates of deceased persons, and handle the adoption and guardianship of minors.)

"We take a dim view of any attempt to shift the ultimate decision-making responsibility away from the duly established courts of proper jurisdiction to any committee, panel, or group, ad hoc or permanent," said the high court. "Thus we reject the approach adopted by the New Jersey Supreme Court in the Quinlan case of entrusting the decision whether to continue artificial life support to the patient's guardian, family, attending doctors, or hospital 'ethics committee.' "

Justice Paul Liakos, who wrote the decision, added:

We do not view this most difficult and awesome question — whether potentially life-prolonging treatment should be withheld from a person incapable of making his own decision — as a gratuitous encroachment on the domain of medical expertise. Rather such questions of life and death seem to us to require the process of detached but passionate investigation and decision that forms the ideal on which the judicial branch of the government was created. Achieving this ideal is our responsibility and is not to be entrusted to any other group purporting to represent the "morality and conscience of our society" no matter how highly motivated or impressively constituted.

Saikewicz died two months after the court's affirmation, of bronchial pneumonia. But though his death was an apparently peaceful one, the attitude of many Massachusetts doctors was not. Upset by the decision, they charged that it meant that judges were, in effect, better doctors than the doctors, and that the probate system was too involved a process for deciding crucial medical issues. Others began practicing intensive defensive medicine — that is, ordering tests and resuscitating patients who had no chance of recovery. One report said that a woman was subjected to cardiac defibrillation — a technique used to normalize irregular heartbeat — seventy times in a twenty-four-hour period before she finally died. Another said that doctors even implanted a cardiac pacemaker in a brain-dead patient (brain death is defined as absence of electrical activity in the brain), so worried were they about letting the patient go without the court's permission.[7]

But while the Saikewicz decision angered and confused the medical community, another decision by the Massachusetts Appeals Court seemed to affirm the right of doctors to enter so-called DNR (Do Not Resuscitate) orders for terminally ill patients without having to go to the courthouse. This case involved a sixty-seven-year-old widow, Mrs. Shirley Dinnerstein, who was suffering from Alzheimer's disease, a degenerative brain disorder for which there is no cure and no treatment that can slow its course. The woman's two children, one of them a physician, agreed with the attending doctors that their mother should be allowed to die peacefully should she suffer a stroke or heart attack. The hospital staff feared, however, that if life-sustaining equipment were withheld, doctors and other personnel might be liable to damage suits alleging failure to provide necessary medical care.

Ultimately, the appeals court ruled that the case did not belong in the courts, and that doctors treating Mrs. Dinnerstein could withhold life-support equipment from her.

How does the Dinnerstein case differ from the Saikewicz case? Why did one case belong in court, and the other not?

The answer, according to Judge Christopher J. Armstrong, was that the Dinnerstein case did not offer a lifesaving or life-prolonging alternative. "It presents a question peculiarly within the competence of the medical profession of what measures are appropriate to ease the imminent passing of an irreversibly ill patient in the light of the patient's history and condition and wishes of her family," said the judge. He added that such a decision was not for judges to make but for a doctor to determine "in keeping with the highest traditions of his profession."

What it all meant was that in cases involving patients like Saikewicz (incompetent, suffering from a treatable condition, with a reasonable expectation of permanent cure or temporary remission of symptoms), the probate court must be petitioned before life-sustaining measures are withheld. In cases like that of Mrs. Dinnerstein (incompetent, suffering from an incurable condition likely to result in death within a year), the doctor, with the concurrence of the family, may issue DNR orders in the event of cardiac or respiratory arrest.

Although these two decisions have resulted in some practical guidelines, at least in Massachusetts, some concern has been expressed by those who believe that family and friends, who once provided support and guidance in such cases, may have been shunted aside by bureaucratic decision-makers. Robert M. Veatch, a professor of medical ethics at the Joseph and Rose Kennedy Institute of Ethics at Georgetown University, is one who feels that way. Writing in a recent issue of *American Medical News*, a publication of the American Medical Association (AMA), Dr. Veatch expressed the fear that "a large and bungling bureaucracy may bury the compassion and common sense that Karen Ann Quinlan and Joseph Saikewicz seem to be crying for." He added the following words, which merit careful attention:

> This talk of courts and committees, of bureaucracies and battles, horrifies those of us who are still worried about caring and compassion. There is a place for both courts and committees. Sometimes both can be helpful, but woe unto us if we as responsible citizens pledged to one another in bonds of loyalty get lost in the maze of feuding bureaucracies. What is missing is an understanding of the proper role of the family and family surrogates, of their rights and responsibilities.
>
> In cases where an incompetent has once been in a position to develop and express his own beliefs and values, who can better be given the first presumption of

knowing those beliefs and values and of taking the responsibility to act upon them than a family member? In cases where the patient has never been competent, the integrity of the family becomes even more central. Courts, committees, hospital bureaucracies must be put to the service of care and compassion that comes from that familial integrity.

The family's task is enormously difficult. The members must make decisions in an institutional setting that is unfamiliar to them. They must deal with technical questions that they often do not understand. The emotional strain is overpowering even when the family is not burdened with guilt in their past relationship with the dying member.

Medical professionals have a grave burden in the face of this central significance of the family. Medical professionals — the nurse, the physician, the chaplain, the administrator — can make the burden lighter. They can encourage active participation of the family in such decisions and support them when the task is the hardest.

When the support of the professionals for the family is present, the courts and the committees that we have feared so greatly should not be a problem. They will intervene in only the most unusual circumstances — when no family member is able to take responsibility and when serious disagreement exists among the parties. To fail to intervene in such circumstances would be irresponsible on the part of society. Committees would be seen as sources of support for decision-making rather than as competitors for authority. Courts would be seen as society's final arbitrator when the family's judgment must be reviewed.

On the other hand, if the family is relegated to the

position of the group clustered outside in the waiting room, then I feel that the courts and committees we have heard so much about will dominate when care and compassion ought to prevail.[8]

We have been discussing, for the most part, cases of dying patients who cannot be saved. But what of patients who can be saved, but who are refused, or refuse themselves, help because of strong religious beliefs? Consider another celebrated Massachusetts case, this one involving Mrs. Eleanor Maurer, thirty-one, who gave birth to her third child, a healthy baby, at Falmouth Hospital on Cape Cod. Later, she began bleeding uncontrollably, a situation that could not be remedied without a transfusion. But the woman and her husband were members of Jehovah's Witnesses, a fundamentalist sect that regards the Bible as the infallible word of God. Beforehand, the couple had signed a waiver absolving the hospital of any liability should a blood transfusion become necessary. The Maurers, like all Jehovah's Witnesses, believed that the Bible prohibits transfusion, as implied in the Acts of the Apostles, chapter 15, verse 29: "That you should abstain from things sacrificed to idols, and from blood, and from things strangled . . ."

When it became apparent that the woman's life could not be saved without new blood, her doctors, aware of the waiver she had signed, asked her if she wanted a transfusion.

"She had a tube going down her windpipe and could not speak," said her husband, "but the doctors asked her yes and no questions and she would blink, once for yes and twice for no, or the other way around, I don't remember, and she definitely indicated she did not want a transfusion. The doctors came out and asked me several times if I would agree to a transfusion, but I did not."[9]

Mrs. Maurer died, and she need not have, according to all of her physicians. "A blood transfusion or two or three definitely would have saved her," one said. "She was totally salvageable except for her beliefs. Blood could have been given with no difficulty at all to save her life."[10]

Her husband's response was terse: "It was God's will."

In similar cases, physicians have often secured court orders to force patients who refuse transfusions for themselves or for their minor children to have them. In this case, there was no time to obtain such an order.

One might argue that Witnesses are exercising their constitutional rights — indeed, in test cases they have brought to the U.S. Supreme Court they have won the right to refuse jury duty, avoided having to salute the flag, and won the right to preach on the streets and solicit house to house. But do they have the right to refuse treatment that will save their lives, basing that refusal on religious freedom?

The answer seems to be that they do have the right to refuse — but that they cannot refuse for their children. "The [first] amendment embraces two concepts — freedom to believe and freedom to act," said one high-court decision in the case of parents who tried to refuse blood for their infant who would have died or been mentally retarded without it. "The first is absolute, but in the nature of things the second cannot be. The right to practice religion freely does not include the liberty to expose . . .

a child . . . to ill health or death. Parents may be free to become martyrs themselves. But it does not follow they are free, in identical circumstances, to make martyrs of their children before they have reached the age of full and legal discretion when they can make that choice for themselves."[11]

Truth-Telling

Most of us have recited the commandment of God, "Thou shalt not bear false witness against thy neighbor," or possibly read the passage in the Epistle of Saint Paul to the Ephesians, "Wherefore, put away lying, speak ye the truth every man with his neighbor, for we are members of one another."

Truth, the cornerstone of human character, a simple noun that exhorts us to perform a most difficult task — being honest. "Do you swear to tell the truth, the whole truth, and nothing but the truth, so help you God?" goes the familiar oath. And we answer soberly, "I do," left hand on the Bible, right upraised. "Cross my heart and hope to die," says a child, promising that what he or she has uttered is unadorned fact.

Indeed, truth-telling is a cherished act, but it is not always easy, or advisable. We often find it difficult to be honest with someone if we know it will hurt that person's feelings, or give that person information with which he or she may be unable to deal. We tell "white lies" about ourselves and our accomplishments when we want to impress someone, embellishing and embroidering the truth in a relatively harmless way.

Truth-telling is one of the dilemmas that confront those who study medical ethics and those who must deal with patients. How much one should tell a patient is the crucial question, and though your first reaction might be, "Of course, tell him or her everything," it may not always be best to do so. On the one hand, it might be argued that the patient has a right to know the details of his or her condition, its degree of seriousness, the side effects of medication, the risks of surgery. On the other, a physician might feel it is his or her duty to withhold information, or to hedge a bit when asked a specific question, because the patient may be unable to handle the information.

Doctors and other caretakers, of course, do not always have access to the real truth. They may not know, for instance, just how long a patient has to live, or if an operation will be successful. In situations like that, when a patient asks for a firm answer, about all a doctor who wants to be honest and tell the truth can say is, "We really don't know," or "Fortunately, you're in good shape, so your chances of pulling through this surgery are fairly good."

But in cases where a physician is reasonably certain that the outcome will be serious and can predict the consequences of revealing such information, he or she is faced with a choice of being totally open with the patient, stretching the truth to take away some of its harshness, or lying outright. The surgeons who answered the aforementioned survey conducted by the American Society of Abdominal Surgeons were also asked if they believed in telling a patient that he or she has a terminal illness. These replies were typical:

"I do not believe in withholding pertinent information from a responsible individual."

"I assess each case. Some you can tell, others no. Some will end up too depressed and that's not worth it."

"No, I don't tell them because I might be wrong."

"Usually, yes. In only one case in 20 years have I failed to do so and then because of some insurance matter. I felt the patient would commit suicide."

"This depends very much on the patient. I ask the family's advice because they usually know him better than I."

"It depends on the nature of the illness."

"If they don't ask me, I say nothing. Do you think I'm going to go marching in there and say to them, 'Hey, you know what, you're dying.'"

"I believe in telling a patient he has a potentially terminal illness, not that he has a terminal illness."

Truth-telling is one of the major concerns in life-and-death cases and, again, circumstances usually govern what a physician tells the patient — whether it's the whole truth, the truth with charity, or a lie. Much is being written today about the dying patient, what he or she thinks and feels when death nears, and more and more caretakers in hospitals are facing the fact that the terminally ill are still human beings who should not be forced to cope alone with their fears and anxieties. But for too long, doctors and others who deal with the dying have avoided discussing their patients' plight with the patients themselves — some-

times out of refusal to accept the defeat that death represents to the healer, at other times because they simply find
it difficult to talk about in a face-to-face situation.

Nowadays, the attitude appears to be that if one is going
to err, it is best to err on the side of information, because
it has been shown that when physicians, nurses, family, or
friends refuse to talk about death to people who are dying
— and especially to people who know they are dying —
the patient's feelings of helplessness and isolation are
magnified. And these feelings, in many cases, are harder
to bear than the threat of death itself. Many patients, of
course, do not want to know the truth, and will not ask
essential questions, and this attitude must be respected.
But for patients who do want to know — and those who
have researched the subject say that most do want to hear
the worst — it is unfair to play a game of deception.

You might ask yourself here if the age of a patient
with a terminal illness would have anything to do with
whether or not it is easier to be candid. Elderly people,
we all suppose, are more aware of death and, therefore,
have the right not to be treated like uninformed children.
But the young, too, are aware of death, and although they
may not always be able to express their feelings, those
feelings are present. The following episode, told at a
National Institute of Mental Health workshop on improving dialogue within families about death, illustrates how
much more a child knows about death and dying than
adults suspect.

A few days before he died, Jamie, a six-year-old, made
a drawing that his mother brought to the physician in
charge of his case. The drawing was in pencil, and it was

of a grave with a cross that was inscribed with the child's name. The boy had also drawn his mother, and in the picture she towered over the grave, looking down on it. Up in the sky, there were clouds, birds flying, and a shining sun with a sad face, and a single tear running down it.

The child was communicating, implicitly asking for some help in lessening his loneliness and fear. He had never spoken of death or of his illness with his mother — who had brought the drawing, out of curiosity, to the physician without fully comprehending the message.

Most mental-health professionals would agree that, as painful as it is for an adult to do so, it is wiser to face a terminal illness and discuss it as fully as possible with a child than it is to hide it behind a smoke screen of denial.

Although how to decide whether to tell the truth to a dying patient is a question that is asked often by doctors and families, the issue of truth-telling also arises in other, less dramatic, cases that force one to make moral choices. Consider the following example, discussed recently at "ethics rounds" at the Children's Hospital Medical Center in Boston. A young patient with kidney disease is a candidate for a kidney transplant, and her father is the only member of her family who would be a suitable donor. The father, however, admits that he lacks the courage to give up one of his kidneys, pointing also to the uncertain outcome for his daughter, and the slight chance that a cadaver kidney might also be used. He decides he does not want to donate, and he asks the doctor to tell his wife and two other children that he is not a suitable donor after all. He fears that if they know the truth about his reluctance, they will accuse him of allowing his daughter to die, and the family will be torn apart.[12]

In this case, the doctor was uncomfortable with the request — but he agreed to tell the man's wife that "for medical reasons" he should not donate a kidney.

Did the doctor act correctly? Was he actually lying when he cited "medical reasons"? Should he have tried to change the man's mind?

Another truth-telling dilemma is illustrated by the following hypothetical case constructed by Dr. Melvin Levine, a pediatrician and assistant professor at Harvard Medical School. An eight-year-old girl, self-conscious about the fact that she wets the bed, is about to go to summer camp. Recently, however, her doctor has started her on medication that seems to control her bed-wetting. She feels good about this, and wants to take the pills at camp before bedtime. But she is a bit embarrassed about even taking bed-wetting medication. She tells the doctor, who suggests that she tell the other children that the pills are just vitamins.

Did the physician act correctly? Was it ethical for him to, in effect, teach a child how to lie? Should he have emphasized that bladder disorders are nothing to be ashamed of, and suggested that she tell the truth about the purpose of the pills? Or should she have been advised that she has a right to privacy and that if anyone asks her about the medication she should say the pills are her business and no one else's?

The following case, as told by ethicist Robert Veatch,[13] is still another example of the complexity of truth-telling in medical matters. A forty-one-year-old woman has unexpectedly become pregnant, and has been referred by her physician to a special genetics unit because she is considered at risk of bearing a mongoloid child. She is eighteen weeks pregnant, which does not leave much time for a potential abortion. The genetic counselor recommends amniocentesis, a test that entails drawing a sample of the fluid that surrounds the fetus from the abdomen with a needle. Microscopic examination of the cells fails to detect the extra twenty-first chromosome that is characteristic of mongolism.

But there is something else — an abnormal makeup of chromosomes. Sex is determined by two chromosomes designated X and Y. Normally, the female complement appears as XX, and the male as XY. But in one of every five thousand male births, the complement is XXY rather than XY, with the error leaning toward femaleness. There is also an error in the opposite direction, XYY, and that situation is often referred to as "supermaleness." This is the difficulty the woman faces. Usually tall and somewhat retarded, XYY males turn up once in every two thousand male adults. The main problem, according to some researchers, is that XYY's tend to be more aggressive than normal males, and inclined to violent acts. Other researchers dispute the connection, saying there is no evidence that such children will grow up to be emotionally disturbed, or criminals.

What, then, does the doctor tell the woman? Does he decide that since there is research suggesting a potential problem he must alert her, pointing out also that there is contrary evidence? Does he keep silent about the matter, reasoning that since no one can agree on the danger of an XYY pattern, he is not obliged to confuse the woman? If he makes a decision to tell the woman all about the difficulty, should he consider whether the woman and her husband will treat the child any differently? Should he consider, further, what impact such information could have on the child himself if he found out about his chromosome balance later on and read or heard about mental patients or murderers who were also XYY males?

Finally, there is this case, as presented by Dr. Levine. A doctor is performing a routine physical examination on a two-year-old child. He decides to give her a mumps vaccination as a precaution. Before the child's mother takes her home, the doctor remembers that he gave the girl a mumps shot just last year. He realizes that the second shot was unnecessary, but that it will not affect the girl in any adverse way.

What should the doctor do? Forget the incident and hope that nothing goes wrong because of the shot? Or tell the mother what he's done and risk losing her confidence in him as the family doctor?

Cases involving placebos raise other truth-telling dilemmas. Placebos are inactive substances that doctors sometimes give patients to lead them to believe that something is being done for them. In fact, placebos — which may be simple sugar pills, starch tablets, or flavored water — are often effective in relieving pain or other symptoms if the patient expects them to. Such a demonstration of mind over matter is one more example of what is known as psychosomatic medicine — the association between mind and body in overcoming and acquiring illness.

But although a placebo might benefit a patient, the question troubling medical ethicists is, Is giving such a "medication" ever justified? Consider the dilemma facing Dr. Brown. His patient is a thirty-five-year-old man who has undergone extensive surgery for a severe back problem. For about a year after the operation, the patient was in great pain, and Dr. Brown prescribed a potent, potentially addictive drug to lessen the pain and help the patient sleep. Eventually, the pain decreased, but the patient needed the narcotic to sleep, and also took it on occasion when he experienced intermittent spells of minor pain. Dr. Brown was concerned that his patient was becoming a drug addict, so he decided on an elaborate ruse to wean him from the narcotic. He substituted a specially prepared capsule that was identical in color and shape to the narcotic-containing capsule. At first, the new capsules given the patient contained the actual drug mixed with a harmless substance. Gradually, however, the narcotic was removed until after a few months, the patient was taking a placebo with the addictive substance wholly replaced by an inert ingredient.

Can one really object to using a placebo in such a situation? After all, the doctor is only doing what he feels is in the patient's best interests, is he not? If he told the patient the truth, wouldn't that ruin any possibility of the deception working? But what of the patient's rights in this instance? Doesn't he have a right to know that the medicine he is taking is pharmacologically worthless and perhaps less costly? Shouldn't he have been warned that he was in danger of becoming an addict and other appropriate steps been taken to help him? Isn't there a possibility that the inactive material in the placebo could have some adverse effect on the patient?

Sometimes, a placebo effect is sought in prescribing active drugs, such as antibiotics. The rationale is that when the patient knows he or she is taking an effective drug it may help, even though the doctors are not sure that it will work in the patient's particular case.

Also controversial is the use of placebos in experiments involving human subjects. For example, researchers may want to compare the efficacy of a new sedative against that of an old one, but they want to rule out chance or the false positive effect that is sometimes brought about merely by giving a drug. So, a group of patients are given the new drug, an equal number are given the old drug, and another group of patients are given a placebo. If the experiment has been conducted properly, the researchers will know with certainty which of the drugs is better; the patients who get the placebo will, under normal circumstances, experience no effect.

Sometimes, such experiments are conducted "blind" — that is, the subjects don't know whether they are getting the real drug or the placebo. Often, though, the experiments are conducted "double-blind" — neither the subjects nor the conductors of the test know.

Is the deception that is going on in such cases of research more or less serious than what goes on when a placebo is given to lead a patient into thinking something is being done for him or her?

A number of ethical problems are associated with the use of placebos in research studies, not the least of which is the matter of informed consent — giving the subject enough information before he or she agrees to go along with the test. Dr. Sissela Bok, a lecturer on medical ethics at Harvard Medical School, tells of a 1971 case involving Mexican-American women who applied to a family-planning clinic for oral contraceptives. Some were given the birth-control pills, others got placebos that looked like the real thing. The reason for this was that, unbeknownst to the women, they were being used in an experiment to determine the side effects of various contraceptive pills.

"Those who were given the placebos suffered from a predictable side effect," said Bok. "Ten of them became pregnant. Needless to say, the physician in charge did not assume financial responsibility for the babies. Nor did he indicate any concern about having bypassed the informed consent that is required in ethical experiments with human beings. He contented himself with the observation that if only the law had permitted it, he could have aborted the pregnant women!"[14]

Bok points out that few physicians appear to consider the implications of informed consent when they prescribe placebos, and their argument is that the usefulness of a placebo may be destroyed if the patient knows too much. The same holds true in many experiments. But Bok argues that there are ways of avoiding deception without abandoning placebo controls in experiments. "Subjects can be informed of the nature of the experiment and of the fact that placebos will be administered," she says.

> If they then consent to the experiment, the use of placebos cannot be considered surreptitious. Although the subjects in a blind or double-blind experiment will

not know exactly when they are receiving placebos or even whether they are receiving them, the initial consent to the experimental design, including placebos, removes the ethical problems having to do with deception. If, on the other hand, there are experiments of such a nature that asking subjects for their informed consent to the use of placebos would invalidate the results or cause too many subjects to decline, then the experiment ought not to be performed and the desired knowledge should be sought by means of a different research design.[15]

Do you agree with that last point? If you do, would you change your mind if the experiment held great promise for the development of a drug that could wipe out cancer — but only if the test could be conducted without giving any information whatsoever to the subjects? How important, in your mind, is informed consent?

As for the diagnostic and therapeutic use of placebos, Bok goes on the presumption that this is undesirable, arguing that by and large, given the principle of informed consent and concern for human integrity, no measures that affect one's health should be taken without explanation and permission. She concludes:

Honesty may not be the highest social value; at exceptional times, when survival is at stake, it may have to be set aside. To permit a widespread practice of deception, however, is to set the stage for abuses and growing mistrust. Augustine, considering the possibility of giving official sanction to white lies, pointed out that "little by little and bit by bit this will grow and by gradual accessions will slowly increase until it becomes such a mass of wicked lies that it will be utterly impossible to find any means of resisting such a plague grown to huge proportions through small additions."[16]

This, of course, is the danger of stretching the truth — or even withholding it — too often. Episcopal theologian Joseph Fletcher, an authority on morals and medicine, talks of the subversive result of occasional lying. "It makes no real difference," he says, "whether it is perpetuated by a direct commission of an untruth, or indirectly through the omission of a truth. Lying troubles the waters of human relations and takes away the one element of mutual trust without which medical practice becomes a manipulation of bodies rather than the care of and for persons. The assumption made by the physician, when he has the *presumption* to withhold the truth, is that the patient is really no longer an adult, but rather either a child or an idiot, more an *it* than a *thou*."[17]

But again, as in all matters involving personal moral actions, it is difficult to practice the ideals that are preached. Dr. Levine has put the dilemma into proper perspective:

I had always been interested in medical ethics but was struck by the incredible discrepancy between the disciplines of philosophy and medicine. A group of philosophers would sit around and say, "Of course, in all medical situations the physician must tell the truth to the patient. No one in society has a mandate to distort the truth." And then I would be with a group of doctors who would say, "Of course you don't tell the truth to the patient when it's going to cause harm. The way that you regulate the truth is critically important in terms of trying to diminish the amount of suffering that people have. Sometimes people aren't ready to hear from us."

And the philosophers would say, "That's subject to terrific abuse. Who do you doctors think you are? When I go to a doctor, I want to know that the doctor's telling me the full truth all the time." And so forth and so on. In issue after issue, one could see that medical practice and much of what was being discussed by philosophers and theologians were diametrically opposed.[18]

Scarce Medical Treatment

An ocean liner has sunk, and the survivors have taken to lifeboats. One of the small boats is capable of carrying only twelve people, but fifteen have clambered aboard. The boat is in imminent danger of sinking unless three of the occupants go overboard. Who goes and who stays? Who decides? How?

The lifeboat story has been told and retold in many ways to illustrate the difficult question, When you can't save everybody, and no one agrees to sacrifice himself or herself to save others, who should be chosen to live and who should die?

The question assumes, of course, that someone will have to be let go, distasteful as the idea might be, and that the good of the greatest number must be considered. But then one must ask, Why are numbers so important? Aren't the individual lives of three people worth as much as the individual lives of the twelve who will be saved? Is life not the most basic of rights?

Granted, each human being has worth. But in our lifeboat analogy, you cannot save them all. And unless you are an extraordinarily doctrinaire individual who believes that if all cannot be saved then all must accept their fate and die, you know that a choice has to be made. But how? Are three of the weakest picked out and forced over the side? The oldest? If it just so happens that there are three idiots in the lifeboat, shouldn't they go? If your country's president and assorted leaders are aboard, shouldn't they automatically be spared? Shouldn't women and children be saved? Should the choice be made randomly, by having everyone draw lots?

The question of how to choose who gets life-saving treatment is one that plagues those who must allocate scarce medical resources like kidney and heart transplants, and hemodialysis (treatment with an artificial-kidney machine that cleanses the blood of toxic wastes). Organs for transplant, and dialysis equipment, are not only scarce, they are quite costly. Not everyone who needs them will get them.

Consider a heart transplant, a drastic procedure that is still far from being routine despite the improvements in the technique and the lengthened life span that may be achieved with the operation. It has been estimated that the number of potential candidates for the transfer operation is as high as forty thousand per year. But the number of donor hearts is extremely limited, obviously because one needs a heart to live, and the transfer, when an appropriate donor can be found, must be done fairly quickly. This contrasts with a kidney transplant, in which the potential recipient may be maintained on a kidney machine until the right donor — who can live with one kidney — is found.

So, a decision has to be made about who should receive the scarce grafts. There are several criteria and alternatives to be considered, one of which is the screening out of candidates strictly on the basis of medical history.

When it has to be decided whether to allot some scarce form of treatment, the decision is often made on the basis of some reasonable benefit to the patient. In the minds of most physicians, for instance, it would be pointless to transplant a scarce heart into a heart patient who also has terminal cancer; the heart could be used to save and extend the life of someone else. Physicians who must make such medical decisions also, on occasion, take into consideration the patient's age and emotional outlook.

Some ethicists, however, raise the question of what, exactly, constitutes a medical benefit. "If it is years of added life," says Robert Veatch, "then children would get the highest priority; the senior citizen would, for all practical purposes, be barred. If the problem of definition could be resolved, medical benefit might be a plausible criterion for allocating resources. However, it still masks a fundamental value judgment, which reflects a medical orientation. To select on the basis of 'strictly medical criteria' is to argue that any amount of 'medical benefit,' whatever that may be, is preferable to an even larger gain that is not medical. This assumption is questionable."[19]

It has also been suggested that one's ability to pay for expensive and scarce resources should be a criterion. How do you feel about this alternative? There is no question that money often does bring one better treatment — not only in hospitals but in the courts, in restaurants, and in doing business. If one has ample cash, is there really anything wrong with using it to one's advantage?

Then there is the matter of the patient's social worth. Does the derelict with no home, no family, and nothing to contribute to society merit a scarce kidney machine in the same way that, say, the Pope or the President of the United States does? Should the widowed father of five children receive the heart transplant before the bachelor who is responsible for no one but himself? Do we rule out the mongoloid child when a choice has to be made about who gets a rare vaccine?

Decisions based on utility are not uncommon. Baseball managers most often use a pitcher with proven ability in a crucial game rather than the rookie with great potential. You, yourself, might give money to a needy organization that helps the poor rather than to a bum on the street. The shortage of penicillin in the U.S. Army aide stations during World War II is often cited as an example of applying the principle of utility. The antibiotic was needed to treat both the wounded and those who had contracted venereal disease. Medical officers often chose to give the scarce penicillin to the soldiers with VD on the grounds that those men would respond to treatment more quickly than the wounded, and thus would be able to return to battle sooner. This same reasoning is applied in disasters when the principle of *triage* is followed — if a number of victims are to be cared for, treatment is given first to those whose ability to function can be quickly restored because their help is essential. The more severely injured are helped later.

But making choices on the basis of social worth — as workable as it is in some instances — presents problems, too. One has to consider the values of the individual who makes the choice. That person's idea of who is socially worthy may not necessarily reflect what is best for society. The decision-maker, for instance, may hate artistic people and see them as dewy-eyed dreamers who contribute nothing useful. The bias might be toward individuals who produce goods or render professional services — physicians, pilots, business executives, carpenters, and the like. A decision-maker's political or religious beliefs could also creep into the process. In the last analysis, we really can't agree — or even know— who is worth more. Because of this difficulty, many ethicists feel that, with the exception of cases like that involving the distribution of penicillin to soldiers with VD, where the aim appears fairly clear, making a judgment on an opinion of social worth is not advisable.

Arthur J. Dyck, a member of the faculty of the Harvard Divinity School, refers to the ideal of the Good Samaritan and an "equality of life" philosophy. "We should minister and care for the maimed, the dying, and the bleeding, and do this without asking any moral questions, other than whether we are indeed fulfilling the law, and whether we are indeed loving God and loving our neighbor," he says. "The moral question for us is not whether the suffering and dying are persons, but whether we are the kind of persons who will care for them without doubting their worth."

Professor Dyck offers that view in contrast to the opposing "quality of life" view of some doctors and ethicists
who base decisions to maintain life on utilitarian grounds
such as social worth, who equate human dignity with
control, and who believe that to be dependent is to be less
than human. He cites pediatrician Alex Haller, who "finds
no difference between the fetus and the newly born, both
being dependent, helpless, and lacking in the dignity that
goes with autonomy or rationality. Whatever we can do
with a fetus (says Haller) we can do with an infant,
because neither has the worth of autonomous human beings." (In a similar fashion, some ethicists have maintained that the severely retarded are not human, that
mongoloids, for instance, are not persons.)

Against such thinking, Dyck points out that the equality-
of-life school recognizes certain time-honored human
rights as basic — life, liberty, and the pursuit of happiness. These, he says, are everyone's and are not based on
the greatest good for the greatest number.

"Life is the most basic right of all," says Dyck. "It is
not to be qualified by another's assessment of the quality
of any individual's life. . . . Because all of us are dependent, sometimes irrational and foolish, there is probably no decent way to draw the line on when we are
worthy humans. Lines will be drawn by the powerful. As
things stand now, it's usually the physicians who decide
who shall live or die. If their decision depends upon their
assessment of our worth, life in our society will be that
much more precarious. If the courts are to decide what
medical practice should be, so much the worse."

What, then, do we do in the lifeboat? On what basis do we decide who is saved and who dies?

Many who have agonized over this decision — including maritime-law authorities, who have, in fact, considered overloaded lifeboats in drawing up rules of conduct — believe that selection must be made on a first-come, first-served basis, or by drawing lots. In other words, in our lifeboat example, the first twelve who make it into the boat stay, the others are turned away, no matter who they are. If fifteen manage to climb aboard, then some sort of lottery must be devised to determine which three sacrifice themselves. This way, the value of each individual's life is considered, not his or her worth to society as defined by another human being.

In the case of allocating a scarce medical treatment, a lottery could also be employed, but only after a medical judgment first screens out those who would not benefit from the procedure or drug.

But — and it seems there is always a "but" in questions involving ethical choices — selection by lot, as fair as it is, means that we might have to abandon our time-honored belief in giving women, children, and people in wheelchairs special attention. Again, circumstances might have to be considered, conditions that might well force us to make exceptions to the rules of even a lottery. It can be argued that there are innumerable instances in which one's decisions to allocate a scarce medicine or piece of equipment *must* be governed by the decision-maker's responsibility to a cause or a policy rather than to an individual patient.

In all fairness, one has to question whether an individual's rights *always* supersede those of the public. In the real world, we are committed to many interests, values, and desires that are for the good of the community at large and without which society could not long survive.

Human Experimentation

In 1900, a small group of U.S. Army physicians and soldiers participated in a daring experiment conducted by Dr. Walter Reed, the famed medical officer. They volunteered to be infected with yellow-fever germs in order that the course of the disease could be studied. Two of the men died as a result of the experiment, which proved that yellow fever was transmitted by the bite of a mosquito.

In 1767, the British medical educator and experimenter John Hunter, then thirty-nine years old, deliberately infected himself with a discharge he took from a patient suspected of having gonorrhea in an attempt to prove that syphilis and gonorrhea were one and the same. Hunter developed the symptoms of both diseases — probably because his patient had both — and concluded erroneously that the two were identical. Hunter was in ill health for the rest of his life, probably because of his self-experimentation.

The history of medicine is full of examples of individuals who volunteered to be human guinea pigs to test a new drug or procedure or to study the effects of a disease. But it is doubtful that those who conducted such experi-

ments in the early days ever bothered to inform the subjects about the risks or, in the case of experimenting on
themselves, submitted their plans to a research investigation committee for approval.

Times have changed, and there is much more concern
over protecting the rights of human subjects who take part
in clinical investigations. Regulations that would provide
stronger protection for subjects involved in research activities are constantly being written and rewritten, and today
most investigators would consider it unthinkable to carry
out a research project on a human being without his or her
consent.

But one doesn't have to go back too far to find abuses
— and even today, in an age of societal concern and
government regulations that respect the rights of human
subjects, evidence of troubling practices occasionally surfaces. There have been complaints among scientists that
the rules by which they must play may interfere with, or
even make impossible to conduct, a given experiment.

Let's examine some of the problems that have cropped
up in human experimentation, and how those interested
in the subject respond to them.

Perhaps the most deplorable examples occurred in Nazi
Germany. Concentration-camp inmates were subjected to
all manner of atrocities in a misguided interest in science
— men and women were left naked in the snow and immersed in ice water to determine how long humans could
survive under such circumstances; they were dosed with
poison gases, shot with poisoned bullets; they were fed
salt water to find out how long they could live without
fresh water; they were held underwater and allowed to

drown, in order that doctors might remove their lungs later to examine the mechanism of drowning.

In a classic account of how a dictatorship can warp medical science, Boston psychiatrist Leo Alexander has told of how one German neurologist received some five hundred brains from Hitler's killing centers for the insane. Dr. Alexander, who was a consultant to the U.S. secretary of war during the Nuremberg trials, quotes the German doctor as saying, "There was wonderful material among those brains, beautiful mental defectives, malformations and early infantile diseases. I accepted those brains, of course; where they came from and how they came to me was really none of my business."

One could argue that the scientists who thought that way were simply acting under the orders of superiors, or that they were guided by a set of official values that, though revolting to the rest of the world, were in force at that time in history in that particular country. Somehow, they, too, became caught up in the appalling insensitivity to humanity that was the hallmark of the Hitler years. Scientific thought, like everything else in Hitler's Third Reich, became highly politicized, and the freedom of inquiry that scientists have traditionally been brought up on was sacrificed for baser motives.

Dr. Alexander points out that in addition to the "material" sought by the German neurologist, a number of other cases were brought in, such as patients with depression and severe mental illness. "These were selected from the various wards of the institutions according to an excessively simple and quick method," said the doctor. "Most institutions did not have enough physicians and what physicians there were were either too busy or did not care, and they delegated the selection to the nurses and attendants. Whoever looked sick or was otherwise a problem was put on a list and was transported to the killing center. The worst thing about this business was that it produced a certain brutalization of the nursing personnel. They got to simply picking out those whom they did not like and the doctors had so many patients that they did not even know them, and put their names on the list."[20]

Obviously, such things as informed consent, potential harm to the subject, and the right of the subject to withdraw from the experiment if he or she chose were never considered by the German experimenters. But the Nazis were not alone in breaching the doctrine of informed consent and the Hippocratic injunction against doing harm to the patient.

Suppose you know that a certain drug will help victims of a specific disease, but you don't give that drug to a patient because you want to know more about the course of the disease. Are you justified in withholding treatment, without informing the patient, on the grounds that even though the patient might die, the information you'll learn about the disease will help others later?

Something like that happened in what has come to be known as the Tuskegee syphilis experiment, begun in 1932 in Alabama with nearly four hundred men. The experiment was designed to determine the long-term effects of VD on untreated victims. All of the patients — all black males, most of whom had less than a sixth-grade education — were persuaded to join a social "lodge" named after a nurse who supervised the study in the field. The U.S.

government sponsored the experiment, and to get the men to join in, offered them free medical care (except for treatment of syphilis), free rides in government automobiles, thirty-five dollars in cash to each participant, inexpensive burials, and free hot meals.

Eventually, the lack of treatment began to take its toll. Four years after the experiment started, heart disease associated with syphilis had infected many of the men. By 1944, the mortality rate for the syphilitics was double that for the control group. But worse than all of this was the fact that when penicillin became widely available, none of the men in the study was treated with it — even though the experimenters knew the drug was effective against the disease. Moreover, though many of the men in the study were in the advanced stages of the disease, they were never informed of the nature of the illness. One report even had it that men who were inadvertently treated by doctors not participating in the study were dropped from the program. By 1972, there were only seventy-four survivors. Each one had some disability that could be associated with untreated syphilis.

Although more than a dozen studies of the experiment were published in medical journals, there were but a few protests. Later, other reports suggested that the study added little to medical knowledge of syphilis.

Some years later, another study, equally questionable, surfaced. It had to do with nutrients and infants, and involved allowing certain children to be starved in order to study the effects. Again, the participants in the study were predominantly black, a fact that prompted the understandable comment from one journalist: "It has become increasingly clear that the most popular practice tools in many laboratory experiments seem to be rats, cats, dogs and black people. . . . Black people [should] be aware that cruel and inhumane experimentation is not a thing of the past. Genocide is a real threat, and don't ever forget it."

In a disturbing report in 1966, Dr. Henry K. Beecher, director of the anesthesia laboratory of Harvard Medical School, at the Massachusetts General Hospital, expressed his concern over experimentation on a patient "not for his benefit but for that, at least in theory, of patients in general." Writing in the *New England Journal of Medicine*, Dr. Beecher presented twenty-two examples of unethical or ethically questionable studies, saying, "It is evident that in many, the investigators have risked the health or the life of their subjects."[21]

Most of the people involved in the experiments cited were charity-ward patients, members of the military, mental retardates, prisoners, and the like — in other words, not the usual private patient. Among the cases Dr. Beecher outlined were these:

• Juvenile delinquents and mental defectives between the ages of thirteen and thirty-nine who were afflicted with nothing more serious than acne were given a powerful drug. The drug, effective against some organisms, also apparently caused liver malfunction. At the end of the first month, liver problems were so widespread that the project was finally halted three weeks later. Although the researchers apparently knew at the end of the first two weeks that something was wrong, they continued the tests on the liver-damaged patients.

• Liver cancer cells were injected into twenty-two persons who were told only that they were getting "some cells." The word "cancer" was left out.

• Subjects with normal hearts were used with sick patients to test a new method of inserting a needle into the heart. The risks were quite unknown and since all of the subjects had normal hearts, they had nothing to gain and all to lose.

• Normal babies were studied to determine whether or not a condition known as ureteral reflux — in which urine backs up from the bladder to the kidneys — can occur in normal kidneys. Twenty-six infants less than two days old were catheterized — a technique that involves passing a long, fine tube through the body and which puts a patient at risk of infection — and x-rays were made of their bladders filling and emptying. Probably no one will ever know the results of the x-ray exposure on the infants.

• One hundred servicemen were given ineffective placebos, while others got penicillin to prevent the development of heart-endangering rheumatic fever. Of those who received the placebos, two developed the fever and another, kidney disease. Those who got the penicillin suffered no such effects.

• Institutionalized mental defectives were deliberately infected with hepatitis, an inflammation of the liver. Although their parents' consent was obtained, a mild epidemic was touched off, and there was no indication in the report that the parents were told about the risks; nor did the experiment take into account a resolution of the World Medical Association that there is no justification for risking injury to one person for the benefit of another.

· An especially deadly cancer known as melanoma was transplanted from a terminally ill child to her apparently well mother in the hope that the mother's antibodies against the daughter's tumor might be effective in her treatment. The daughter died the day after, however. The implant was removed from the mother after a month, and she died a year and a half later — of melanoma.

"Human experimentation since World War II has created some difficult problems with the increasing employment of patients as experimental subjects when it must be apparent that they would not have been available if they had been truly aware of the uses that would be made of them," Beecher said. "Evidence is at hand that many of the patients in the examples never had the risk satisfactorily explained to them. And it seems obvious that further hundreds have not known they were the subjects of an experiment, although grave consequences have been suffered as a direct result of experiments described here."

Patients, he said, will usually go along with just about any request a physician makes of them, based on trust. "At the same time," he added, "every experienced clinician-investigator knows that patients will often submit to inconvenience and some discomfort, if they do not last very long, but the usual patient will never agree to jeopardize seriously his health or his life for the sake of science."

In only two of the fifty examples originally compiled for Beecher's study was consent mentioned. "In any precise sense," he said, "statements regarding consent are meaningless unless one knows how fully the patient was informed of all risks, and if these are not known, that fact also made clear." In the military studies cited, the young men did not know, were not informed, and did not consent. They weren't even told they were subjects in an experiment.

In the last analysis, Beecher said, one should not take great risk for frivolous ends. "The gain anticipated from an experiment must be commensurate with the risk involved."

The use of prisoners presents special problems, if only because the subjects represent a captive group. "It is a difficult situation," said Beecher. "The very invitation to participate may function as a bribe, if the rewards are excessive. This, then, destroys the whole concept of free consent."

The idea of performing medical experiments on volunteer prisoners is not a new one. According to the World Health Organization, as long ago as 1721, King George I of England offered a free pardon to inmates of a London prison who submitted themselves to smallpox inoculation. Commented WHO:

> Six prisoners volunteered, and the question arises: was this experiment ethical by modern standards? And there is the collateral question: was the consent of these prisoners "informed," "valid," "true," and "free"? For these prisoners, such questions would have seemed very

pedantic, for by volunteering all saved their necks, won their freedom, and acquired a new immunity to a highly dangerous disease that was then a universal threat. Such an example must give rise to doubt about the validity of the widely accepted view that consent is not "informed" if the person consenting is motivated by the expectation of receiving some benefit not directly related to the experiment. Is there any essential difference in the case of such consent and that of the many who accept hazardous employments for high wages?[22]

One must also question whether it is possible, given the conditions existing in most prisons today, to make use of the informed-consent doctrine.

"Information about the experiment can be provided by the researcher, but a judgment about an acceptable degree of risk requires contact with the free world as opposed to the prison environment," observed Dr. George Bach-y-Rita of the University of California in a report in the *Journal of the American Medical Association.* "What may be perceived as an acceptable risk for a person inside a prison may be totally unacceptable for that same person outside. Lack of unimpeded access to information, absence of advice from a physician friend of the prisoner's own choosing, lack of legal counsel, censorship of mail, and the long-term isolation from the changing ideas of society greatly restrict the prisoner's ability to evaluate the magnitude of his risk and thus to make an informed decision about a research contract."

Dr. Bach-y-Rita said also that another difficulty is the lack of meaningful employment for prisoners, a situation that makes it easy to coerce them into taking part in a medical experiment — the lure of a little pocket money is all it takes to secure a subject. "Coercion as an institutional policy is incompatible with research," said the doctor. "When information regarding a person's participation is used in formulating decisions about a prisoner's degree of freedom, research is not possible. In every instance, responsibility ultimately rests with the investigator. It is he who must assure that conditions compatible with current social mores are present prior to starting a project."[23]

And nowhere are problems with social mores encountered more often than in experiments at the other extreme of life — the human fetus. For certain kinds of medical research, the use of human tissues is essential, and the lost or discarded fetus is an obvious source of such material, because it has the same organs and nervous and circulatory systems as a full-grown human being, only smaller and less developed. These are things that no experimental animal has.

Many people are shocked that human fetuses are used in such a way, but as Dr. Leon D. Sabath of Boston City Hospital's Channing Laboratory once said in defending his participation in an experiment to detect the amount of antibiotic passing into a fetus: "When you see a child with a congenital defect, or a person, possibly someone in your own family, with cancer — unsolved problems now — think of how these problems might be solved, partly by research on the fetus."[24]

An important question to ask here is: Should an aborted fetus be regarded as a dead person, and be treated with all the respect that is due the dead — or should we regard it as a sort of tumor or parasite of the womb of the woman who conceived it? It has been argued that an aborted fetus, whether temporarily alive or already dead, is not injured, or subjected to pain, when it is used in an experiment. If this is the case, why shouldn't it be a research subject that might provide us with answers about how various diseases start and progress?

Again, we must concern ourselves with deeply ingrained emotional attitudes. There are many who view the fetus as a human person, and its deliberate destruction as murder. Physicians, theologians, lawyers, and social scientists engage in heated arguments that grow in intensity each time abortion becomes a public issue. Proponents of abortion argue that the fetus is not a human being, scientifically or legally, because it cannot live without its mother, cannot sue for damages in a court of law, and cannot inherit an estate. Its destruction might be considered an act of mercy, they say, both for the good of society, and for those directly concerned. Abortion is also regarded as a matter of self-defense, if the mother's life is at stake.

It is not our purpose here to go deeply into the abortion debate. But the subject of experiments on human fetuses does necessitate some discussion.

Many researchers feel, as does Dr. Sabath, that the health of future generations might be improved by fetal research. "If physicians were ever to be denied the ability to perform autopsies responsibly and properly for research purposes on human remains once life has departed, a substantial segment of essential medical research would no longer be feasible," said Dr. Michael J. M. Dykes, a senior scientist in the AMA's Department of Drugs, and

Dr. Emily E. Czaoek, of the Department of Pediatrics of Northwestern Medical School. "Such research is essential to the understanding and eventual control of the factors that cause congenital malformations [birth defects] and, having been instrumental in the development of prophylactics [vaccines] for polio, measles and German measles, has already contributed much to human welfare. Although we are unalterably opposed to wanton desecration as opposed to decent disposal of human remains, including those of fetuses, we urge that physicians not be forced to cease studying such remains in a reponsible and a proper manner."

Society cannot have it both ways, the two doctors said. "It cannot demand drugs that are safe, including safe for pregnant women and unborn fetuses, and at the same time unreasonably restrict responsible and proper research on human remains, including and especially abortus research."[25]

Still, the issue is a controversial one, and those who are against such research are not willing to concede that the survival of the human race is at stake if fetal experimentation is prohibited. The problem, they contend, has been compounded by the U.S. Supreme Court's ruling legalizing abortion, which, obviously, makes fetuses available to researchers. It is serious enough, say the opponents, for a scientist to experiment on a fetus that is dead when it is removed from the womb, but more so for him or her to work with a fetus that has been kept alive for long periods of time, as has been done in some institutions. Moreover, they feel that those who experiment on living fetuses should be prosecuted. Fetuses cannot give consent, and, say opponents of abortion, experimenting on them bears remarkable similarity to the experiments on mentally defective children carried out in Nazi Germany in the 1930s.

Said Boston City Councillor Joseph Tierney, who took a strong stand some years ago against experiments with human fetuses at Boston City Hospital: "I propose that when an abortion produces a live or viable fetus, every measure should be taken so that the fetus at least has a chance for life. I strongly urge that this be guaranteed by enacting legislation that would require the presence of such external life support systems and medicines in the place where abortions take place. Under no circumstances should a fetus, a potential human being, be kept alive simply and solely for the purpose of human experimentation, and such a practice should be prohibited by law."[26]

Several states now have laws regulating fetal research, prohibiting research on live human fetuses — that is, those that show evidence of heartbeat, movement, or electrical activity in the brain — and allowing experiments on dead fetuses.

The American Medical Association's policy on fetal research allows a physician to participate in such work, but sets up a number of guidelines. For example, if appropriate, studies on animals and nonpregnant humans should precede fetal research projects; there should be no monetary payment to any legally authorized representative of a fetus to obtain any fetal material; informed and voluntary consent should be obtained in writing from a legally authorized representative of the fetus.

"The purpose of the research," say the guidelines, "is

the production of data and knowledge which is scientifically significant and which cannot otherwise be obtained."

It is difficult to argue against the contention that there may not be a suitable animal model for a particular disease under study. Even where animal experimentation is possible, there comes a time when tests must be done on humans. One can also understand the fears of scientists that the horror stories about human experimentation make it impossible to conduct even the most innocuous experiments, something that could severely hamper the quest for knowledge.

Says Dr. Pierre Soupart of Vanderbilt University, "In any kind of human-subjects research, the only way to determine the validity of the research proposal is by balancing the risks against the potential benefits. You don't get anything for nothing. So you must decide whether the benefits from the new knowledge justify the risks you take to get the knowledge."[27]

[3]

Lawful Killing

———•◆•———

Most of us would agree, I think, that we have the right to defend ourselves or our private property from attack by using force, provided we do not use more force than is necessary. The expression "kill or be killed" holds true under some circumstances, and justifiable homicide, as it is called, allows a police officer to kill a fellow human being if duty requires it, or allows any one of us to take the life of someone else in self-defense. Under such circumstances, no legal guilt is incurred, and the perpetrator — unlike someone who commits a premeditated murder or kills someone in the heat of passion — may be excused.

Under the law, however, we may not take a life if we can safely retreat from the attacker. Similarly, killing to protect private property is not justified under any circumstances.

The law also allows the state to take a criminal's life after due process of law. And, under international law, governments are allowed to wage war, which necessitates the taking of enemy lives.

War and capital punishment raise a number of moral

and ethical questions. When, for instance, are they justified? Are they ever justified? Is a conventional war — that is, one not fought with nuclear weapons — more moral than one fought with them? Does the way in which a convicted criminal is put to death make capital punishment more or less acceptable? Who must bear the ultimate responsibility in war? The government that wages it? The scientists who develop the terrifying weapons? The soldier who carries out his country's orders? May a soldier disobey an order he considers unjust or immoral? In executing a criminal, does the executioner bear as much responsibility as the state that permits the death sentence?

War

A word can touch off a war, or an impulsive finger on the firing button of a nuclear-tipped missile, or an attack-predicting computer gone haywire. Hunger and oppression and religious fervor can do it; so, too, can greed for territory and power. A nation may be forced into a war to defend itself, or may start one simply by punishing, with the use of deadly force, a grave act that some country has committed against it, or against its citizens. In Greek legend, Helen, wife of Menelaus, King of Sparta, eloped with Paris and triggered the siege and destruction of Troy; in 1914, in Sarajevo, capital of Bosnia, an archduke named Francis Ferdinand and his wife were shot to death by a member of a secret society in an assassination that plunged all of Europe into war.

Branded as the greatest of all crimes and the business

of barbarians, war is fire, famine, and pestilence, carnage and suffering. A monumental human tragedy, it is a public and state act, as distinguished from the acts of private individuals, and although it operates under the aegis of a government of laws, there is no law that can prevent it. Because it has been with us for so long, at least since the days of Ninevah and Babylon, and the delta tribes of the Euphrates River, four thousand years before Christ, it almost appears to be essential, as paradoxical as that may seem, to survival. "War is a continuation of politics by other means," said Karl von Clausewitz, the Prussian military theorist whose ideas greatly influenced the German military before and during World War I. In his *Summa Theologica,* Saint Thomas Aquinas, the Italian philosopher and theologian, said that although peace was humankind's greatest goal, it also had a duty to defend the state. And the Spanish Jesuit theologian Francisco Suarez taught that wars are not evil in themselves; that just wars could be fought provided there was no other way to achieve justice; that they must be waged by lawful authority; and, finally, that war must be conducted and peace imposed with moderation.[1]

As horrible as war is, it is fought — or, let us say, it is supposed to be fought — under all sorts of rules and regulations. Under the Geneva Conventions, the first of which was signed in 1864, and the Hague Peace Conferences, in 1899 and 1907, provisions are made for the humane treatment of prisoners of war and the wounded, for the protection of civilians and hospitals and medical transports. There are regulations prohibiting the use of asphyxiating gases and expanding bullets, the bombardment of undefended, or "open," cities, and the taking of private property by an invading army without compensation. And under one provision of the Hague Conventions, the signatory powers agreed that before war actually begins there will be an explicit warning "in the form either of a reasoned declaration of war or an ultimatum with conditional declaration of war." There are international laws that forbid warring parties to send troops into neutral territory, that define a country's air and sea space, and that guarantee the safety of ambassadors.

But rules, as the popular expression has it, are made to be broken, and virtually every one of the rules of war has been broken — by this nation as well as every other that has engaged in warfare. On December 7, 1941, Japan violated international law by its sneak attack on the U.S. naval base at Pearl Harbor, Hawaii. During World War II, the Nazi government in Germany murdered millions of Jews, and forced people from European countries to work as slave laborers in war factories. The Soviet Union, a long time after World War II, still refused to repatriate prisoners of war. During the Korean War, the Chinese Communists and the North Koreans reportedly subjected many United Nations soldiers to cruel and abusive treatment. And during the Vietnam War, there were instances in which United States soldiers and airmen massacred civilians and sprayed tons of toxic chemical defoliants over jungles and crops to prevent the enemy from hiding and from replenishing food supplies.

Each of those acts was, and may still be, excused by someone on the grounds that feelings of anger, fear, and aggression run high in wartime. The belligerents, more over, are always convinced that their side and cause are right, and that they may use all the force and means they have to destroy, do harm to, or demoralize their enemies. Mistreating prisoners of war, killing civilians, attacking without warning, and the like, may all be condoned by those who believe that the end can justify the means, no matter how severe those means, or that wartime is abnormal and thus combatants and civilians alike should not be expected to act as they would under normal circumstances. Therefore, the rules of war may be broken. Even in situations where extreme cruelty is used, one can argue — and feel comfortable in doing so — that when the enemy are ruthless, they are to be given a dose of their own medicine. Such feelings are understandable, but may be carried too far.

Nowhere was this better exemplified than in the celebrated case of Lieutenant William Calley during the Vietnam War. Calley, a young officer in the United States Army, was accused of killing, or causing others to kill, a total of 109 "Oriental human beings, occupants of the village of My Lai 4, whose names and sexes are unknown, by means of shooting them with a rifle."[2]

The victims of the massacre were defenseless and unresisting civilians — old men, women, children and babies. Some of them were thrown into ditches and machine-gunned, others were clubbed with rifle butts. The expression "Waste them" was heard often over the bursts of fire. Buildings were blown up and burned, frenzied soldiers bayoneted cows — and when the horrible affair was over, many of the soldiers reportedly bragged about how many "gooks" had been killed. It was, without doubt, one of the most despicable incidents in U.S. military history, one that would confuse and trouble Americans for years to come.

Calley testified at his court-martial that he was taught to suspect all the Vietnamese he encountered, that he was to "forget the World War II notion of giving candy and chewing gum and things to children," that he wasn't curious about what his men were shooting at as they moved through My Lai. He said also that his superiors had pressured him to come up with "high body counts," and, in what has probably become his most often quoted comment, declared that he had not informed his company commander about the shootings because "there wasn't any big deal."

Calley also argued that he was following orders, that his commander, Captain Ernest L. Medina, gave those orders to kill all the villagers — a charge that the commander denied. "Such an order would be so flagrantly in violation of the laws of war, to say nothing of common humanity, that Calley could hardly have taken it seriously unless it was in keeping with his prior military experience," said General Telford Taylor, a professor at Columbia University and an authority on international and criminal law. "If it was in keeping, he might well have done as he did without any explicit instructions from Medina. If not, the order should at least have puzzled and disturbed him, which plainly was not the case."[3]

When Calley's trial was over, six officers — five of whom had served in combat in Vietnam — agreed that he had violated the laws of land warfare, found him guilty of premeditated murder, and sentenced him to life in prison. (The sentence was later reduced to twenty years.)

Incredibly — or maybe not, when one considers the divisions that arose in America over the Vietnam War, and the belief that soldiers must do their duty — there was a furor over the Calley verdict. Many Americans were sympathetic to the young officer, declaring angrily that he was singled out for punishment, that others involved had gone free or were simply reprimanded. And others — more than one cares to admit — defended Calley's actions, saying that the officer was only doing what he should have done under the circumstances, and that they, too, would shoot unarmed civilians if ordered to do so in the sort of war Calley was involved in.

Whether such a view reflects actual callousness on the part of American citizens or was simply their way of defending their pro-government position with regard to the war is hard to determine. Many people had misgivings about the Vietnam War, but went along with it because, in the words of American naval hero Stephen Decatur, "Our country! In her intercourse with foreign nations may she always be in the right; but our country, right or wrong."

It was difficult for many who supported the war to be suddenly told that Calley was wrong in doing what he did, and that they, in effect, shared in the responsibility for his actions.

Even President Nixon must have felt that Calley had been wronged. Nixon freed him from the army stockade in which he had been held, while his lawyers appealed the case, Later, the President added that he would person-ally review the case, no matter the results of the appeal, in a "non-legal, non-technical" manner.

But not everyone was sympathetic. In a letter to Nixon, Captain Aubrey M. Daniel III, the prosecutor in the Calley trial, declared:

> How shocking it is if so many people across this nation have failed to see the moral issue which was in-volved in the trial of Lieutenant Calley — that it is unlawful for an American soldier to summarily execute unarmed and unresisting men, women, children, and babies.
>
> But how much more appalling it is to see so many of the political leaders of the nation who have failed to see the moral issue or, having seen it, compromise it for political motive in the face of apparent public displea-sure with the verdict. . . .
>
> I have been particularly shocked and dismayed at your decision to intervene in these proceedings in the midst of the public clamor. . . .
>
> Your intervention has, in my opinion, damaged the military judicial system and lessened any respect it may have gained as a result of the proceedings. . . .
>
> For this nation to condone the acts of Lieutenant Calley is to make us no better than our enemies and make any pleas by this nation for the humane treatment of our own prisoners meaningless.[4]

Most discussions of the Calley case allude to the so-called Nuremberg Trials held in Germany in 1945 and 1946, in which an international military tribunal — including the United States and its allies in World War II — charged a number of individuals with a variety of crimes and atrocities. Among the charges against Nazi military, industrial, and political leaders were: the deliberate instigation of aggressive warfare, extermination of Jews, murder and mistreatment of prisoners of war, and the use of slave labor.

Many of the defendants argued — as did Calley — that they were not legally responsible for their acts because they were merely performing them under orders of superior authority. However, the tribunal rejected this argument, saying that although this circumstance might be considered, it was not a defense in international or domestic law. "The true test," said the tribunal, "is not the existence of the order, but whether the moral choice [in executing it] was in fact possible."

Twelve defendants were sentenced to death by hanging, seven were sent to prison, and three were acquitted. One, Hermann Göring, the commander in chief of the German air force, committed suicide in prison a few hours before he was to be hanged.

Several questions are raised by all of this. Should U.S. leaders have been put on trial along with Calley for the atrocities committed in Vietnam? If the Nazis were convicted of, in effect, not rebelling against unjust and immoral orders, shouldn't we understand the feelings and actions of those who were against the war in Vietnam and who refused to serve in the military? In 1973, for example, a young B-52 bomber pilot, Captain Michael J. Heck, refused to fly a bombing mission over North Vietnam because "the goals do not justify the mass destruction and killing." The same year, another American pilot refused to fly a mission over Cambodia because, as he put it, "The destructive power B-52s unleash is totally unnecessary in that war." There were other, similar cases during the Vietnam War, and it was the air force's general policy to discharge such pilots under "other than honorable circumstances" instead of bringing them to court-martial. Can't we, then, justify anyone's refusing to obey what he or she considers to be an unjust or immoral order about anything?

Americans bombed civilians during World War II, and so, too, did the British and our other allies. If we had lost the war, would the Germans and the Japanese have been justified in trying our leaders and hanging them? Or were we justified in killing civilians — who might well have had no real animosity toward us — on the grounds that they probably were supporting the war effort by working in their nation's war factories and turning out weapons meant to destroy us?

The comment of author Michael Novak during the Calley incident is worth mentioning here:

> We were in a quicksand set for us by the Viet Cong. We embraced their rules. No doubt, the American people did not want to know exactly what we were doing in Vietnam. No doubt Presidents Johnson and Nixon wanted to win the war. And General Westmoreland obeyed his mandate to destroy the V.C., while losing as few American lives as possible and not going into North Vietnam. No doubt soldiers in the field, who saw many buddies bleed their lives away on inhospitable soil but

who seldom if ever saw a living enemy soldier, learned all too well the rules of "people's warfare." Moral judgment in the concrete situation remains a bucket of worms.[5]

Capital Punishment

The death penalty for committing a crime is the harshest punishment that human beings can inflict on one of their kind. It has been with us, in some form or other, since ancient times, and has been meted out for offenses as trivial as spreading false rumors (in India), for murder, and for conspiring to transmit U.S. atomic secrets, in wartime, to the Soviet Union, as in the case of Julius and Ethel Rosenberg in the 1950s.

In recent years, in countries other than the United States, hundreds of people have been shot, hanged, and had their heads lopped off for terrorist acts, dope dealing, embezzlement, murder, homosexuality, adultery, rape, and political crimes. The last execution in the United States (at this writing) occurred in Indiana in 1981. There are about five hundred inmates on Death Row in this country, most of them in the thirteen southern states. Except for a few special cases, all fifty states have abolished the mandatory death penalty for murder, rape, and other crimes, and the decision between capital punishment and life imprisonment has been left to the discretion of juries or the court. This results from the U.S. Supreme Court decision in 1972 that the death penalty, when imposed mandatorily by a jury, for murder and rape, constitutes cruel and unusual punishment, and violates the Constitution's Eighth and Fourteenth amendments.

In 1976, the high court ruled that the death penalty did not violate the ban on cruel and unusual punishment, but did say that mandatory death sentences are not valid. At the same time, the court upheld death-penalty statutes passed in three states — Georgia, Florida, and Texas — but struck down those of Louisiana and North Carolina. At this writing, thirty-five states have enacted capital-punishment laws that have not been successfully challenged in the courts. Does capital punishment deter one from committing a crime? If you knew that you could be executed for drinking before the legal age, wouldn't you think twice? But, then, don't the Ten Commandments tell us not to kill, and isn't that rule violated when we put someone to death? Does the nature of the crime have anything to do with how you feel about capital punishment? Is a mass murderer more despicable than a spy? Do you see any difference between executing a convicted murderer and killing the owner of an enemy weapons factory?

Those who would retain the death penalty argue that it prevents some people from committing crimes, that it saves the public the expense of keeping an offender in prison, that it is more humane than life in prison, and that it is the just desert of one who breaks the divine law against murder and takes a life that is sacred — as the Book of Genesis puts it, "Whosoever sheddeth man's blood, by man shall his blood be shed."

Said Monsignor Thomas J. Riley, former rector and professor of moral theology at St. John's Archdiocesan Seminary in Boston, "The supreme authority of this state has the right to inflict the death penalty when it can be shown to be a necessary means for protecting society against criminal attack which endangers its very foundations. Society has not yet reached the stage of moral development at which it would be prudent to remove a safeguard judged to be necessary by so many charged with the heavy responsibility of protecting life against criminal attack." The monsignor, who emphasized that his opinions were personal ones and not the official Catholic position, concluded that it would be wrong to consider capital punishment a violation of the laws of God.[6]

Opponents of capital punishment do not believe that fear of death stops a person from killing any more than the prospect of life imprisonment does. Generally, statistics collected when capital punishment was more widely used show murder rates about the same in states that have abolished capital punishment. Wisconsin was often used as an example. Between 1941 and 1946, the state, which did away with the death penalty more than a hundred years ago, had an average rate of 1.5 murders per 100,000 population. Neighboring Illinois, which had the death penalty at the time, had a corresponding rate of 4.4.

Abolitionists have argued that most murders are committed in the heat of passion by family members or close acquaintances, and that such crimes — with no premeditation — thus could not be prevented by fear of execution. It has been said that if the death penalty were imposed for ignoring traffic lights, that offense would probably never be a law-enforcement problem again — but murder, no.

Murder rates also differ from country to country because of ingrained attitudes toward violence, and they differ because of living conditions. Some murderers may be driven to kill as a result of brain chemicals gone wrong, or even by the weather, and putting someone to death for committing a crime under the effect of what is temporary insanity is surely unjust punishment.

Another argument against capital punishment is that the months and years condemned men and women often spend on Death Row while their sentences are being appealed leave them spiritually and mentally scarred. There is also the argument that a convicted person might be mistakenly executed for a crime he or she did not commit. And there is the argument that the death penalty is most often imposed on those who are poor and friendless, or members of minority groups. People of means, it seems, seldom go to the electric chair or the gas chamber.

Finally, the death penalty is criticized as a barbaric rite, morally indefensible, that brutalizes society by cheapening life, and leaves us breeding cruelty with more cruelty. Vengeance is its reason for existing, some say, not the deterrence of crime or a desire to do public justice.

One must ask whether capital punishment can have any value whatsoever. For instance, what does it do to correct the one who performs a wrongful act? We punish a child, or reprimand an employee, not to remove pleasure from him or her, but to demonstrate the error of their ways. A dead person cannot be rehabilitated. Nor can we use capital punishment to educate the public because then we are saying that one form of premeditated murder is all right, while another is anathema.

Earlier, we asked whether the form that warfare takes

makes it any more abhorrent, or whether the way in which a convicted criminal is put to death makes it more or less acceptable. Recently, four states — Texas, Oklahoma, Idaho, and New Mexico — adopted laws requiring that a lethal dose of a drug be injected into a condemned criminal. Several other states are considering this new method of capital punishment whose goal is less painful and more humane treatment for the prisoner. Other reasons for using the method, however, might be to encourage juries to opt for the death penalty, and to save money with a cheaper way of doing the job. The courts might also be less apt to strike down a lethal-injection law on the grounds of cruel and unusual punishment because supposedly a drug injection is not as barbaric as hanging, electrocution, or beheading.

Among those who have objected to this new way of administering capital punishment are a lawyer and a physician from Harvard Medical School; both recently called upon the medical profession to formally condemn all forms of medical participation in its use. Particularly offensive to William J. Curran, a professor of legal medicine, and Ward Casscels, a physician, is the requirement in the laws that the lethal dose be prepared, administered, and monitored by medically trained personnel. In an article in the *New England Journal of Medicine*, the two said that such involvement would represent "a corruption and exploitation of the healing profession's role in society" and would violate worldwide ethical principles of the medical profession.

The authors conclude that participation of physicians or any other medical personnel "in carrying out a death sentence by intentional skillful injection of a medically prepared substance into the veins of a prisoner seems to us to constitute a grievous expansion of medical condonation of and participation in capital punishment." They believe that a doctor "should not escape moral responsibility by ordering a subordinate to do what he or she may not properly do directly. . . . For physicians to monitor the condemned prisoner's condition during the drug administration and to carry on this action to pronounce death when heartbeat and respiration were found to be absent . . . would be so intimately a part of the whole action of killing as to deny any consideration as a separate medical service."[7]

Said Curran:

> No medical practice act of any medical or allied health profession licenses its members to kill. If the medical profession refuses to cooperate with these laws, then it would effectively nullify them, since nurses and other health personnel can only act on the direction and under the supervision of physicians.
>
> We believe that not only the medical profession but also legal experts, legislators, corrections officials and ethicists should seriously examine the issues raised by the new laws. There are a large number of people subject to execution under them — 140 in Florida and 119 in Texas, for example.

The authors point out that while none of the laws requires that a physician personally administer the lethal dose directly into the prisoner, "the degree and scope of medical involvement in this new procedure for execution is greater and more intimate for physicians than any other in medical history." The doctor's participation can range from "ordering the substance and preparing it for injection, to injecting the substance or ordering and supervising the injection by other medical personnel, to monitoring administration and observing the prisoner throughout the continuous injection of the drug, and examining the prisoner and pronouncing his death."

Curran and Casscels cite the Hippocratic oath as the earliest foundation for their opposition. "I will use treatment to help the sick according to my ability and judgment," it says, "but never with a view to injury and wrongdoing. Neither will I administer a poison to anyone when asked to do so nor will I suggest such a course."

Involvement of physicians in the torture of prisoners has existed throughout history and in many different countries, the authors point out. Some physicians in Nazi Germany served as executioners of German sailors and "performed harmful practices and clinical experimentation on the inmates of the concentration camps and prisons," as has been already noted. According to Russian author Aleksandr Solzhenitsyn, doctors in Soviet prison camps were accomplices to interrogators and executioners, and signed death certificates giving the cause of death as "cirrhosis of the liver" or "coronary occlusion" in cases where prisoners had been beaten. In recent years, torture of prisoners has been documented by Amnesty International in Chile, Iran, Paraguay, Portugal, and Argentina. As a result of some of these activities, the World Medical Association's Declaration of Geneva in 1948 and the Declaration of Tokyo in 1975 reiterated the pledge against using medical knowledge "contrary to the laws of humanity."

American physicians, too, Curran and Casscels add, have on occasion violated the federal Constitution by assisting the interrogators of accused prisoners, sometimes by conducting physical examinations to certify that a person either is fit to be questioned or is not under the influence of drugs; sometimes by pumping out the stomachs of arrested persons to recover drugs or other contraband; and sometimes by operating to remove bullets against a prisoner's will in order to have the bullets examined in connection with a crime.

Ask yourself: Should they?

[4]

Ethics in Business and Government

—————•—•—————

You are the president of a large electronics company that conducts a good deal of business overseas. One of your customers is a country that tolerates, but is not especially fond of, the United States, and has, in fact, sided with several other countries against a strong ally of the United States.

Your company, which pays many tax dollars to the United States, needs the business, and continues to sell equipment to the semihostile country, equipment that is used in guidance systems for missiles that would be used against America's ally in the event of war.

Should you stop selling to the country, a move that would be in the best interest of your country's ally — or should you keep doing business briskly, reasoning that if your company doesn't make the profit, a competitor will; that if you quit, you'll deprive your government of tax revenue; and that no threat is aimed directly at the United States because of the sales?

You're a secretary to a U.S. senator, and you discover that he is skimming money from a fund that was supposed to be used exclusively for his reelection campaign; he is diverting it to his personal checking account. He is a popular senator who has been instrumental in securing the passage of important social legislation, and is well liked by minority groups and the poor. If you expose his dishonesty you will undoubtedly injure his chances of re-election, and thus deprive the nation of a well-meaning leader. What do you do?

You are the operator of an amusement park that has not been doing as well as it should because of high costs. You are offered new roller-coaster equipment, which you desperately need, by a manufacturer who wants your business. But you've been warned by other businessmen that his equipment is sometimes unsafe, because to save money he pays little attention to quality control. Do you buy his equipment because it's so much cheaper and might enable you to turn a profit at last?

Your company owes the Internal Revenue Service five thousand dollars in income taxes, a sum that was due three or four years ago. Through some computer mix-up, the IRS has not only missed catching the debt, but now sends you a letter informing you that the U.S. government *owes you* five thousand dollars for that year and will be sending you a check. There is probably no way the government will discover the mistake, so, do you accept the money? Or do you inform the government and pay up?

Some of the most trying moral dilemmas arise in doing business, and in dealing with or working for government.

The profit motive and the quest for power are strong drives that are often coupled with the prevalent notion that business executives and politicians are expected to cheat, at least from time to time. That notion is only strengthened by the many reports in the media and by our own observations of those around us. There were lawbreakers in high places during the Watergate scandal, men who lied, bugged offices, destroyed important documents, fabricated elaborate cover stories, committed burglary, and assumed powers they were never given by the electorate.

President Nixon, as we all know, was forced to resign because of the Watergate disclosures and because of pressures from his colleagues who felt that the nation could only be served by his stepping down. "Richard Nixon did not fall from power," said the *New York Times*. "He slid, gradually, certainly, in a steady corrosion of his realm."[1]

There are drug companies that make false claims for their products, public-relations specialists whose prime job it is to see that only information favorable to their clients is published or broadcast, American companies that invest heavily in African nations that separate blacks from whites in a policy known as apartheid, the FBI's "dirty tricks" campaigns of smearing the reputations of such people as Martin Luther King, Jr., bribery charges not uncommonly brought against congressmen, lawyers who decline to make public the illegal conduct of the companies they represent, presidents and senators who withhold federal funds from states that do not support U.S. policy and dispense it to states that do, economic advisers who minimize or alter unemployment statistics in order to help the candidacy of their contender for public office, drug treatment program officials who inflate the numbers of heroin addicts in a given city so that the mayor will approve an increase in funds to fight the problem. Honesty may, indeed, be the best policy, but one doesn't have to look very far to find out that not everyone — in fact we might say that practically no one — practices the adage all the time.

People cheat regularly in small ways — a slug in a pay telephone, parking at a meter that's stuck in the "on" position, grabbing up a loaf of bread that they know has been erroneously labeled with a low price, using someone's ID card to get a discount in a store that's for members only, or to obtain an illegal drink. In fact, a recent study at the University of Michigan Institute for Social Research demonstrated that nearly half the subjects were willing to cheat on a test when given the chance. Said Lynn R. Kahle, the researcher who conducted the study: "They do manipulate their environment to make it more compatible with their own preferences, desires, needs, traits, attitudes and characteristics."[2]

People cheat regularly in large ways, too, as we've noted in some of our previous examples, and sometimes they do it with less guilt than they would have if they cheated in minor ways. For instance, few business executives would dream of bilking someone out of a few dollars if they were making a personal sale. But many see nothing at all wrong with cheating thousands of customers out of the same dollars by artificially inflating prices. There is also a notion prevalent that putting one over on the government — for example, cheating on income taxes — or on big business is okay.

But is it? Isn't deducting a nonexistent item on an income-tax statement as dishonest as taking home an expensive article that has been priced cheap through error? But what if you're poor, in the case of the cheaply priced bread, say? Shouldn't you be allowed to take advantage of someone's error, someone who can certainly afford it? In the case of the businessman who cheats on his income-tax deduction, couldn't he argue that the system we live under makes such behavior possible by not tightening up the rules, and by making the tax load too heavy to begin with?

Why do business people and politicians cheat on occasion?

The answer is, probably for the same reasons we cheat on tests or in supermarkets or at parking meters. Each one of us probably has a private code of ethics that does not see certain acts as wrong, no matter what we are told. And it is probably true that the fear of getting caught is what keeps many of us from doing a lot of things that are prohibited by law or by moral codes.

Businessmen might argue that they are dealing with such large sums of money that a few dollars here and there are meaningless. Politicians may feel that to bring about some of their campaign promises — actions that will benefit the public — they must make payoffs of some sort or other to states or to high officials. Some businessmen and politicians may be dishonest because they are inept — that is, they cannot achieve the desired ends by doing their jobs properly, so they cheat.

Jeb Stuart Magruder, who was the deputy director of the committee for the reelection of President Nixon, gave his reasons for participating in the planning, execution, and attempt to cover up the Watergate affair to a Senate committee investigating the scandal. It was a classic example of letting the end justify the means.

> I had a course in ethics under William Sloane Coffin [the Yale University chaplain], whom I respect greatly [Magruder said]. He was quoted the other day as saying, "Well, I guess Mr. Magruder failed my course in ethics," and I think he is probably correct. . . . During this whole time in the White House we were trying to succeed with the President's policy. . . . I knew he was trying to settle the war issue and we were all at that time against the war. . . . We saw continual violations of the law done by men like William Sloane Coffin [who was active in the antiwar demonstrations]. Now he tells me that my ethics are bad and yet he was indicted for criminal charges. . . . He recommended that students burn their draft cards, shut down the city of Washington. He was a very close friend of mine. . . . I saw people that I was very close to breaking the law without any regard for any other person's pattern of behavior or beliefs. . . . Consequently when these subjects came up and although I was aware they were illegal, we had become inured to using some activities that would help us in accomplishing what we thought was a cause, a legitimate cause . . . that is an absolutely incorrect decision . . . but that is why that decision was made . . . to all of us who had worked in the White House there was that feeling of resentment and of frustration of being unable to deal with issues on a legal basis.[3]

One might protest, as did Coffin later, that all law-breakers cannot be lumped together, that many of those who participated in the antiwar movement were protesting what they felt to be illegal laws whose legality could be tested only by refusing to obey them. There is an enormous difference, Coffin pointed out, between being a loyal servant to the U.S. Constitution, and being a loyal servant only of the man who hires you.

"If there are differences in ends, so there are differences in means," the chaplain observed.

> Whatever Dr. [Martin Luther] King and Dr. Spock [the famed pediatrician turned antiwar activist] did, they did openly. All America could see and judge. Jeb operated behind closed doors. Most of the people in the civil rights and anti-war movements were careful not to infringe on the civil liberties of other citizens. Jeb and his friends deliberately violated these liberties. When the Supreme Court declared against him, Dr. King went from Georgia to Alabama to take his punishment. The draft resisters who went to jail accepted theirs. But Jeb's crowd, far from accepting punishment, tried only to conceal their crimes. Dr. King and those who followed him disobeyed the law to protect it. It is a sad and savage irony if Government officials learn from the practitioners of civil disobedience that law is made to be circumvented. . . . We have the opportunity to learn from him the ancient lesson that to do evil in this world you don't have to be evil — just a nice guy, not yet a good man.[4]

Lawbreakers in business and politics often defend their actions by saying that there are varying scales of morality, each one dependent on the times. By this reasoning, an act that is less unethical in a time when no one is paying much attention to such matters may become unethical on a day when some major scandal hits the newspapers. This is known as the rationale of moral climate. One could argue, then, that a caveman who killed his neighbor over a minor squabble was not as guilty as a modern-day murderer because primitive people probably accepted such behavior more readily. So, too, did a number of politicians argue in the post-Watergate climate, when virtually everyone was made aware of lawbreaking and immorality in government, that what seemed wrong after Watergate would not have been judged so harshly before the scandal.

One must ask whether such an argument is valid. Is it true that people can become so angry and suspicious after a major scandal surfaces that they overreact to a slight infraction and blow it all out of proportion? If so, then doesn't it follow that some so-called crimes may not be crimes at all? And wouldn't such an overreaction make it difficult for anyone, businessmen and politicians included, to function in the practical world?

It's easy to conclude, against this background of immorality in business and politics, that one way out of the dilemma is to adopt stringent regulations. No one has suggested anything as simplistic as a law based on the honor code of West Point cadets, which says, "A cadet will not lie, cheat, or steal, nor tolerate those who do." But every so often someone suggests laws that would cover all forms of business and all sorts of political activities.

We all know that how a society is regulated depends a good deal on the fundamental values of its members, and our laws are based on these. But laws must be enforced, and this can be done only by appropriate government agencies. The problem with this is that our agencies cannot possibly watchdog every act injurious to our society. So, more laws are passed, and more agencies are set up to enforce them.

"The end result," says Earl W. Kintner, a Washington attorney and former chairman of the Federal Trade Commission, "is authoritarianism, a society in which every significant activity is subject to direct governmental regulation. Such a result is of course antithetical to democratic principles."[5]

What is appropriate in our democratic society, however, is private enforcement of codes of ethics that have been created by society.

"Codes can stimulate the self-regulation and education of industry members and can serve to greatly minimize the need for further pervasive governmental regulation which destroys individual freedoms, individual initiative, and the private enterprise system," says Kintner.[6]

And with regard to ethics in government service, it has been pointed out that those who enter it must be willing to abide by special rules that do not apply to work in the private sector. These rules, says Andrew Kneier, an official of Common Cause, a national citizen's lobby, are necessary to ensure the objectivity of public servants and promote public confidence. Moreover, the fact that some good people — such as experts from certain industries — may go elsewhere, says Kneier, is the price that must be paid for strong policies on conflicts of interest and government integrity.

"There are tradeoffs involved," he says. "On balance, though, it appears the public's interest is better served through measures that prevent government officials and employees from having private interests in the public issues they must decide."

One might argue that all these codes and regulations will not always be acceptable to all individuals, who are human beings with human failings, and who make decisions knowing full well that no matter which course is chosen when it comes to a dilemma, someone will be upset by the decision, or some moral law will be violated.

West Point cadets have cheated in the past and will do so, undoubtedly, in the future, honor code or no. Since dilemmas are often, as we have said, conflicts between two rights, and everyone has a different view of what right is, getting total agreement on a code of ethics is difficult.

It is one thing to say that people must abide by certain rules, and that privately enforced codes can lessen the need for government regulation. But it is another, as those who break the Ten Commandments quite regularly can attest, to say that such codes will wipe out unethical conduct.

[5]

Ethics in Science
and Technology

————•◦•————

In 1980, Pope John Paul II concluded a visit to France with an ominous warning: "The future of man and mankind," said the pontiff, "is radically threatened, in spite of very noble intentions, by men of science."

He singled out genetic manipulation — the altering of the tiny heredity-bearing units found in every living thing — and nuclear weaponry as areas of grave concern, saying that one was as dangerous as the other.

The Pope was not, and is not, alone in expressing such a view. Many scientists and laypeople are alarmed or uneasy about researchers' fantastic ability to construct and reconstruct living matter in ways that will affect our lives and the lives of future generations, and about the dreadful power we have set loose from the atom.

Biologists actually are able to build genes from the chemical ingredients that make up those genes in nature; they can take the genetic material, DNA, from different organisms and splice it together, creating something that never existed before in nature. They can "harness" bacteria, turning them into chemical "factories," and let them manufacture the hormone, insulin, necessary to treat some diabetics; or interferon, an exciting anticancer substance. They can fertilize a human egg with sperm in a glass laboratory dish, implant the egg in a woman, and allow a baby to be born. They can remove an unfertilized egg cell from a frog, destroy its DNA-containing nucleus with radiation, then remove the nucleus from a cell in a tadpole's intestinal tissue and transplant that into the egg cell with the missing nucleus and watch the egg divide and form a complete tadpole exactly like the one that owned the transplanted nucleus.

Physicists can build nuclear reactors that can drive submarines for thirteen years without refueling, or produce electricity to light our homes and power our utilities. Physicians use radioactive materials to diagnose and treat disease; such materials even fuel artificial hearts and pacemakers to stimulate the contractions of a real heart. Physiologists and neurologists can electrically stimulate the brains of human beings to change emotion, relieve pain, or influence memory and speech.

But while all these accomplishments are designed to safeguard our health and welfare and make our lives more comfortable or productive, each has enormous potential for misuse — and it is this potential that gives rise to the many ethical questions associated with what have come to be known as the scientific disciplines of human engineering and high technology.

No matter his or her good intentions, couldn't a researcher accidentally flush an experiment down a laboratory drain, and turn a bacterial Frankenstein's monster loose on the world? In the wrong hands, couldn't the techniques of gene-copying and cloning — manufacturing an exact copy of an individual — be used for evil purposes, such as creating a race of drones? Would the rights of test-tube babies be the same as those of the natural-born? What of the risks in dumping hazardous wastes from chemical plants that produce products absolutely essential for life in a modern-day society? Are those risks worth taking if they mean future Love Canals? (Love Canal is the Niagara Falls site where chemical dumping has raised concern over possible chromosome damage to residents of the area, and the possibility of birth defects and miscarriages.) Do the risks inherent in nuclear energy — the nuclear-reactor accident at Three Mile Island is a case in point — outweigh the benefits?

Underlying all these questions is perhaps the most important question: Even though scientists are now able to do remarkable things, should they? That question is plaguing scientists, ethicists, and the lay public more and more as advances in biology and technology are recorded almost every day. And as they do in every controversy, extremists turn up on both sides of the question. There are those, on the one hand, who would halt all genetic manipulation or who would shut down all nuclear power plants and stop all work with nuclear energy. At the other extreme are those who believe that since science is a never-ending quest there should be no holds barred, and research must proceed at all costs. And, as always, a third view holds that while the risks are there, they can be minimized by the proper safeguards and controls.

Let's consider three major areas of concern — genetic engineering and biohazards; the method of reproduction known as *in vitro* fertilization; nuclear energy and the problems of nuclear waste disposal.

Genetic Engineering

Imagine traveling down the beam of an electron microscope, into the smallest basic unit of life, the cell, a teeming mini-world of incredible complexity. It is a watery place where the cell's many components float about, not purposelessly like so much debris on a tossing sea, but with a goal — the production of vital proteins that will be used by the cell itself and by other cells.

Next we look into the cell's nucleus, the rounded body that contains the chromosomes that are sectioned into the genes that determine inherited characteristics — eye color, body build, and sex, to name but a few. But look even closer, at the gene itself. We see that it is made up of a very long, slender, and twisted substance wound around an inner core of protein. This substance is DNA, deoxyribonucleic acid, the master chemical that carries all the hereditary information in every living thing.

In 1944, a group of scientists at the Rockefeller Institute demonstrated for the first time that DNA carried genetic information; they did this by extracting it from a bacterium. About ten years later, Dr. James D. Watson, a Harvard biochemist, and British physicist Francis Crick finally described for the scientific world the way DNA actually looked and worked. It turned out to be an intricate molecule, a double helix, or twisted ladder, a spiral staircase of chemicals with the uncanny ability to unhinge itself each time a cell begins the division known as mitosis. As a cell divides and duplicates itself, its DNA does too. The result is that each new cell has its own DNA ladder in a new set of chromosomes, and each ladder is packed with the same coded genetic instructions that its parent had because all of the rungs — they're composed of just four chemicals — are arranged in the same precise sequence. It is important to remember that whatever form life takes on this earth — human being, tarantula, or microbe — it is always composed of the same four chemicals: adenine, guanine, cytosine, and thymine. It is the order in which this four-chemical formula is arranged that determines what form life will take.

In the 1950s, someone discovered that DNA was found not only in the cell's nuclear control center, but in other parts of the cell as well, especially in plasmids, tiny circular particles that float free in the cell cytoplasm. Since this free form of DNA is not trapped in the highly organized machinery of the nucleus, scientists can get at it easily, and this is particularly true of the plasmids in bacteria. They are not only accessible but — and for genetic engineers this is their most important quality — they can glide smoothly into other bacteria. Once inside, they duplicate as their bacterium host divides and redivides.

Scientists next made another important discovery that would make genetic manipulation nearly as easy as splicing two ends of a rope together. They purified a special enzyme that has been called a "chemical scalpel" because it can cut the fine bits of DNA into neat pieces. Without this chemical cutting tool, any attempt to chop up DNA would ruin it. The "chemical scalpel," moreover, has another valuable quality. When it is used to slice up DNA, the segments it produces acquire sticky ends. This means that when the experimental researcher slices a specific bit of DNA out of, say, a plasmid from a bacterium and then mixes it with DNA cut from a virus, the sticky ends of each DNA segment glue together. When that happens, something new has been put together, a new genetic package fused from two bits of DNA from different sources. This tiny new product, known as recombinant DNA, may then be slipped easily into other bacteria, and as those bacteria multiply by dividing, each new cell produced contains recombinant DNA that is identical to that made when the original bits were glued together. The technique is so simple that any high-school student could do it, as long as he or she had the special enzyme that acts as a chemical scalpel.

Thus, scientists can now take genetic material from two different sources, tie it together, and then grow as much of it as desired. The recombinant genes, no matter how many are made, will still act as they did when they were first joined. For example, if a researcher transferred plant genes that make chlorophyll to a bacterium of a different species, that bacterium would then be able to make chlorophyll, something it could not do in nature.

This moving about of genes between organisms that had little genetic contact in the past has caused a good deal of excitement among biologists and industrial chemists who hope not only to learn more about the structure of genes and how they work but to see enormous practical applications in work with recombinant DNA.

"A new breed of entrepreneurial researchers is stalking the chemical and allied industries," said a recent report in *Chemical and Engineering News.*

> The entrepreneurs are practitioners of the new biology — those who use a wide range of methods, including the now familiar recombinant DNA, or gene-splicing technology for the genetic engineering of organisms. The new industry founded by these entrepreneurs already is expanding rapidly. And, proclaiming that the tools at their disposal are powerful, energy-efficient, and reliable, this band of corporate biologists is seeking to challenge a range of industries, reaching beyond producers of commodity and specialty chemicals to manufacturers in the pharmaceutical, food processing, energy-related, and agricultural industries.[1]

Let's consider for a moment what this new industry — some companies have already been nicknamed "gene machines" — is planning and, in some cases, has already accomplished.

Agriculture is one area in which genetic engineering is tremendously valuable. Food supplies are essential to humanity, and in order to improve their quality and quantity, plant biologists have, for years, used crossbreeding techniques. About a hundred years ago, the Austrian monk Gregor Mendel hybridized plants — crossbreeding, or mixing, dwarfed plants with tall ones, and red-flowered ones with white-flowered ones — by transferring the reproductive pollen from one variety to another. He planted the seeds from these hybrids and discovered that each new plant had inherited certain traits as complete units, and that these units (we now know them as genes) were passed along in pure form to subsequent generations.

Various methods of hybridization are used today, but each depends on a recombination of genes. One example is found in the tobacco industry. Plant biologists know that resistance to a disorder known as mosaic virus disease is found in plants that do not have desirable leaf qualities, but that plants with good commercial leaves are susceptible to disease. By repeated crossbreeding of the resistant types with the commercial variety, a tobacco leaf that is both resistant to disease and commercially desirable has been created. In many cases, hybrids are stronger than either parent plant, and this phenomenon, known as hybrid vigor, has been used to increase yields of crops such as corn.

Now that scientists are able to identify which genes are responsible for a plant's special characteristics, their hope is to improve other plants by giving them certain genes. For instance, genes from plants that possess nitrogen-processing ability might be transferred to vegetables that do not, so that the vegetables would no longer require huge amounts of expensive fertilizer. Or, the genes that prevent certain fruits from freezing in wintry weather — such fruits often aren't palatable — might be transplanted into a tree that bears tasty fruit but is not frost-resistant. The result would be frost-resistant fruit that tastes good.

No one seems to object to crossbreeding plants or tinkering with their genes and recombining them with others, and it is doubtful that any serious ethical questions could be raised about such experimentation. Plants are, of course, alive; they have cells and chromosomes, they need food, they grow organs and tissues, and they develop disease. But unless you take to heart Emerson's description of a weed as a plant whose virtues have not yet been discovered, or the tree that Kilmer endowed with a hungry mouth and a nest of robins in its hair, any further similarity to humans is more rhetorical than scientific.

Questions are raised, however, when one begins talking about fusing DNA from two strains of bacteria, or recombining the genes of mammals, the category that includes human beings. Consider the widespread use of *Escherichia coli* bacteria in DNA experiments. Because it is so common in humans and in other animals, fish, and insects, and because it so easily exchanges genetic information with other germs, *E. coli* has great potential for wrongdoing. Suppose a certain combination of genes produced a lethal poison, and this was inserted into *E. coli*. The *E. coli* would multiply rapidly, and so would the poison — and if the organisms escaped from the laboratory and into the city's sewer systems where other *E. coli* thrive, the problems that might arise would be on a par with those that could be touched off by a faulty nuclear reactor.

Or take the case of genes that are blueprinted to resist drugs such as penicillin, a natural occurrence that is the reason why so many germs are now becoming resistant to common drugs. Genetic engineers can insert those genes into bacteria that ordinarily would be killed by antibiotics, and thus create more diseases against which there would be no defense. Transferring a frost-resistant gene to a fruit that does not have one is not the same as slipping an antibiotic-resistant gene into a potentially dangerous germ.

And consider the genetically engineered strain of bacteria called *Pseudomonas,* which is "trained" to devour environmental pollutants such as oil spills in the ocean. All well and good. But what if an oil-sopping *Pseudomonas* somehow got loose in the oil tank that fuels your home, or in the hydraulic system of an airplane, in an oil-storage depot or an automobile's lubrication system? All a *Pseudomonas* "knows" is to eat up oil; it may not care where it is.

There is no doubt that recombinant DNA technology can and will work many wonders to benefit society. Genetic engineers can now make human insulin, the hormone required by many diabetics to control their disease, by isolating the gene that produces it and growing it in *E. coli.* If all goes as scheduled, large quantities of insulin produced in this way will be available soon. No one questions that this would be of enormous benefit to diabetics. Another example is the manufacture of interferon, a scarce virus-fighting substance. Produced naturally in the human body, it has long interested researchers. The substance has been studied since its discovery in 1957, but scientists have had trouble isolating it in the quantities they need to test it as a possible weapon against cancer and other diseases. Until recently, interferon could be produced only through expensive and time-consuming tissue-culture methods, harvesting it from white blood cells that had been exposed to a virus. But in January of 1980, investigators with Biogen S.A., a Geneva-based firm specializing in gene-splicing, extracted genetic material from human cells responsible for manufacturing interferon. The team copied the genes and inserted them into bacteria, which then produced the substance. Clinicians have hailed the achievement, pointing out that the process will drastically reduce the cost of a dose of interferon.

In other experiments, scientists at the Australian National University and the University of California at San Francisco recently gave bacteria special genetic instructions that made the microbes produce large quantities of beta-endorphin, a natural brain hormone with actions similar to those of morphine. Manufactured normally by the pituitary gland at the base of the brain, the substance has been the subject of intense scientific interest because it affects behavior and pain sensation. But in the past it could be produced only by costly and laborious chemical synthesis, and only in small amounts for research. If larger quantities of the hormone can be produced, scientists will be able to test it more thoroughly in human patients, in whom it has already been found to be effective as a painkiller, and may have value as a treatment for depression and schizophrenia. Moreover, its effects on the intestine may make it a useful remedy for diarrhea.

According to Dr. John D. Baxter, head of the California team of researchers, the gene-splicing method used opens exciting possibilities for creating new drugs. The genetic instructions given to the bacteria, he points out, can now be modified to produce a number of different endorphin-like products, including many that would be new to science. This potential may be especially important in developing useful drugs from beta-endorphin, he added, because there is some evidence that the hormone may be more effective when its chemistry has been altered.

Ever since the work with recombinant DNA began, scientists have questioned its safety. In 1978, after months of debate, the National Institutes of Health issued strict guidelines covering potentially dangerous recombinant DNA research, banning, among other activities, the transplanting of genes that produce poisons into common and harmless bacteria, and experiments that could make deadly germs resistant to drugs used to fight them. The guidelines also specified that other potentially dangerous experiments had to be performed with weak organisms that would not be able to survive in the outside world if they did escape from the laboratory. Finally, the guidelines restricted the experiments to so-called clean rooms with double doors and ventilation systems that would filter all the air that left the lab.

Thus far, there have been no major accidents involving recombinant DNA research, a fact that has heartened many of the scientists who were originally somewhat uneasy about the experiments. As a result of the clean record, the guidelines have been relaxed, and more and more chemical companies have entered the new "industry of life." Said Dr. Grady F. Saunders, a biochemist at the M. D. Anderson Hospital and Tumor Institute in Houston:

> There has been much concern about whether "recombinant DNA" research is potentially harmful and whether it should be classified as a biohazard, with national and perhaps international laws or guidelines governing its use. A substantial amount of research on risk

assessment has not shown recombinant DNAs to be more dangerous than the organisms from which they were derived. In fact, recent reports from the National Institutes of Health demonstrated that some DNA tumors' viruses were far less infective when [part of recombinant DNA] than as purified viral DNA. This suggests that the safest way to study extremely hazardous viral nucleic acids is by recombinant DNA techniques. These techniques can be applied to cancer research. The next five years in cancer research should be even more exciting than the last five years.[2]

As more industrial chemists have entered the new growth industry of genetic engineering, their companies have been seeking protection of the rights of ownership of any product that the gene-splicers create. Just as an author may copyright a book, or an inventor patent a tool, so, too, say the scientists, may a genetic engineer own a new life form he or she constructs with a chemical knife. But can a live, human-made microorganism be patented? Should it be?

On June 16, 1980, the U.S. Supreme Court answered the first question in the affirmative. In a five to four decision, the high court ruled that life created in a laboratory is patentable like any other invention. The decision came in a case involving a patent application filed by the General Electric Company in 1972; and the life form involved was a kind of bacterium that had been genetically altered by microbiologist Ananda Chakrabarty to consume oil slicks.

The court's ruling held that test-tube life may be included in the federal law that allows patents for someone who "invents or discovers any new or useful process, machine, manufacture or composition of matter." A living organism, wrote Chief Justice Warren E. Burger in his majority opinion, can fit the law's definition of "manufacture" or "composition of matter." Said Burger:

> The relevant legislative history also supports a broad construction. . . . In 1952, when the patent laws were recodified . . . Congress intended statutory subject matter to "include anything under the sun that is made by man." This is not to suggest that [there are] no limits or that [the statute] embraces every discovery. The laws of nature, physical phenomena, and abstract ideas have been held not patentable. . . . Such discoveries are "manifestations of . . . nature, free to all men and reserved exclusively to none."
>
> Judged in this light, [Chakrabarty's] microorganism plainly qualifies as patentable subject matter. His claim is not to a hitherto unknown natural phenomenon, but to a nonnaturally occurring manufacture or composition of matter — a product of human ingenuity. Congress is free to amend [the law] to exclude from patent protection organisms produced by genetic engineering.

As anticipated, the decision touched off a storm of criticism. Even before it was handed down, an organization known as the Peoples Business Commission (PBC), which has led opposition to all forms of genetic engineering, filed an *amicus curiae* brief opposing the granting of patents to private corporations for laboratory-created, genetically engineered forms of life. (*Amicus curiae* means literally "friend of the court," and refers to someone not a party to litigation who volunteers or is invited by the court to give advice upon some matter pending before it.)

"We believe that it is not in the public interest to allow giant corporations to patent life itself," said Ted Howard, co-director of PBC. "Patenting any form of life, even a microorganism, sets a precedent which will one day be extended to higher forms. We are on the threshold of allowing big business to create, manipulate and own life as if it was merely a manufactured product. This goes beyond the brave new world imagined by Aldous Huxley."[3]

Until the high-court ruling, the only living organisms considered patentable under congressional legislation were certain types of seeds and plants. This was allowed in an effort to encourage plant breeding and the development of new types of crops with desirable characteristics. But, said the PBC, the availability of plant patents has led to the systematic, and irreversible, elimination of many varieties of useful plants and crops simply because they were products of nature and thus could not be patented. This pattern, PBC fears, may be repeated if other forms of life are deemed patentable. The following warnings, from PBC's brief, are essential to this debate:

> The novel microorganisms that will be created through various genetic engineering techniques may well be, in many cases, "superbugs," that is, they will be bred or engineered in such a way that they may become the dominant form of life within their niche in the ecosystem. The General Electric Pseudomonas, for in-

stance, is acknowledged to contain properties resulting from the combination of a number of other bacterium [*sic*]. Once these microorganisms are unleashed into the ecosystem, on purpose or by accident, they may outcompete other forms of life because of their unique properties. This could seriously damage the vitality of the gene pool.

The monoculturing of certain types of high-yield, but disease and pest susceptible plants, will be repeated by the genetic engineering industry through the mono-culturing of "superior" microorganisms. Geneticists are currently predicting, for instance, that within the near-term future, various chemicals, hormones and drugs will be solely produced in the laboratory by genetically engineered microorganisms because such techniques are "cost-effective." Thus, within the foreseeable future, the world will be dependent upon a very limited number of biological entities to produce vital medicine and chemical necessities. The monoculturing of microorganisms may well prove as deficient as that already acknowledged in food crops.

If patents are extended to genetically modified higher organisms [such as domesticated livestock] . . . there can be little doubt that the full history of the patenting of plants will be repeated. One can anticipate that a small number of cattle genotypes [the hereditary make-up of an organism] will be widely reproduced because of their "superior" characteristics; other, less useful, cattle will become extinct; the diversity of the animal gene pool will be as narrowly defined as that now existent among corn, wheat and so on. Dr. Clement Markert of Yale, for instance, is working on methods for the asexual production [cloning] of domestic livestock such as cattle and sheep. In *Fortune* magazine Dr. Markert was quoted as saying: "I could wipe out all of Yale's deficits with the valuable bulls raised from the embryos I could produce in one weekend." That may well be the case, but the fact remains that any such attempt will seriously and irrevocably disrupt the gene pool.

Finally, the history of domestic plant patenting is particularly relevant . . . because many of the very same companies that have gained control of the world's food germplasm are also those now engaged in micro-organism genetic engineering. . . . There is no reason to believe that these companies will develop the genetic engineering life form industry any differently than they have already done in the area of patentable plants.[4]

Among the biologists who opposed the Supreme Court decision was Dr. Jonathan King of the Massachusetts Institute of Technology. "Forms of life," he said, "be they microbial, plant or animal, provide the underpinnings that support life. They are too important to be allowed in private ownership. The patent process protects private gain, but what we must protect is public benefit."[5]

Said Justice William Brennan in the court's minority opinion:

I agree that the question before us is a narrow one. Neither the future of scientific research, nor even the ability of respondent Chakrabarty to reap some monopoly profits from his pioneering work is at stake. . . . The only question we need decide is whether Congress intended that he be able to secure a monopoly on the living organism itself, no matter how produced or how used. . . . Given the complexity and legislative nature of this delicate task . . . we must be careful to extend patent protection no further than Congress has provided.

We are not dealing (as the majority opinion would have it) with the routine problem of "unanticipated inventions." Congress specifically excluded bacteria from the coverage of the 1970 Act. . . . The court's attempts to supply explanations for this explicit exclusion ring hollow.

It is the role of Congress, not this court, to broaden or narrow the reach of the patent laws. This is especially true where, as here, the composition sought to be patented uniquely implicates matters of public concern.

But although Chief Justice Burger considered the issue of public concern and acknowledged that opponents had raised a "gruesome parade of horribles," he added: "These arguments are forcefully, even passionately, presented. They remind us that at times human ingenuity seems unable to control fully the forces it creates — that, with Hamlet, it is sometimes better to bear those ills we have than fly to others we know not of." However, said the chief justice, the granting or denying of patents on microorganisms is not likely to put an end to genetic research — or to its risks.

And there the matter lies. No one can predict just how much of an effect the court's decision will have on recombinant DNA technology, or how many commercial products will emerge as a result. But, to cite one example, already Eli Lilly and Company has announced it has begun limited testing in healthy human volunteers of biosynthetic human insulin produced by genetic engineering. The firm has also begun construction of the world's first manufacturing facilities — at a cost of forty million dollars — to employ recombinant DNA technology to produce the insulin.

Lilly, which developed the first commercial production of insulin from animal pancreas glands in 1923 and has been a major supplier since then, feels strongly that the public will benefit, in light of the fact that forecasts of long-range supplies of animal pancreas glands suggest that animal insulin could likely be in very short supply in about twenty years.

"With the potential availability of Lilly biosynthetic human insulin," said board chairman Richard D. Wood, "we can now see the promise of a time when supplies of insulin will always be adequate to meet public needs. Biosynthetic human insulin is an encouraging example of the way in which new scientific knowledge, such as recombinant DNA technology, can lead to products which serve the public interest."[6]

The debate undoubtedly will go on. Is the research worth the risk? Do the ends — curing disease, sopping up oil spills, manufacturing lifesaving drugs more cheaply, improving crops — justify tampering with Mother Nature's ways? If scientists can make a bacterium do something good, something it has never done before, what's to stop them from making one do something bad? If we can make a germ eat up an oil slick, why can't we just as easily make one that will erode human intelligence in a given race of people?

There is no question that the risks are there. But so, too, are the benefits. We also cannot deny that we are now living in a new biological and chemical age, that we do have more scientific knowledge than our ancestors, that we have evolved. The choice, it would seem, is to forget all of that and go backward, or to proceed, but with caution, aware that there are perils but that they are not all potentially devastating.

In Vitro Fertilization

In the summer of 1978, the world's first test-tube baby, Louise Brown, was born in England. Her method of reproduction is known technically as *in vitro* fertilization (*in vitro* is Latin for "in glass," or in the test tube), and with it has come another biological revolution that has raised a host of ethical and legal questions.

In vitro fertilization is remarkably simple. A physician locates an egg in a woman's ovary with a laparoscope, an instrument that enables the practitioner to see inside the woman's body. The egg is removed with a suction device and allowed to mature for a few hours in a solution in a laboratory dish that has been placed in an incubator, a small chamber that maintains the optimal temperature and humidity for growth and development. Next, drops of sperm, the male fertilizing cells, are added to the dish. The fertilized egg begins to divide and redivide, just as it does *in vivo* — that is, "in the living body" — and when it reaches the so-called blastocyst stage (a cluster of cells) it is implanted in the mother-to-be's uterus. There it grows into a fetus, culminating in birth.

The technique does not always work, nor is it by any means considered routine. Nevertheless, it does offer hope for many couples who cannot have children because the women have blocked Fallopian tubes — the ducts that connect the ovaries to the uterus and through which the fertilized egg travels on its way to the uterus, where it implants itself and grows into a fetus under normal conditions.

A more common method of reproduction is artificial insemination by donor (A.I.D.), a technique that also raises a number of ethical and legal concerns. If, for example, a husband is infertile — that is, his sperm are either inactive or in short supply — sperm are taken from an anonymous donor and deposited in the woman at the height of her fertile period. The donated sperm, which are often frozen and kept in sperm banks until needed, perform exactly as they would during normal intercourse, fertilizing the egg and starting pregnancy.

Still a third method — which has not yet been done in a human — is called embryo transfer. This entails transferring a fertilized egg from one female to another. The technique has been used successfully in cows, pigs, baboons, and sheep. In 1973, a calf was grown in this way from an embryo that had been removed from its mother and frozen for a week before it was implanted in another cow. The calf, a Hereford bull, was born at an agricultural research station in England, and was the first large animal ever to be developed from a frozen embryo. Two years later, the first nonhuman primate infant, a baboon, was produced by embryo transfer at the Southwest Foundation for Research and Education in San Antonio, Texas. A male, it weighed 30.6 ounces at birth and seemed to be perfectly normal. In other instances, prize cows have been made to produce several eggs by giving them hormones, and the animals then inseminated with sperm from prize bulls. The fertilized eggs are flushed out of the cow's womb and transferred to cows without pedigree, in an effort to produce more prize animals.

As in the vast majority of experiments involving biological manipulation, the scientists working with new methods of conception are not part of some diabolical conspiracy. Their goals are commendable ones. Test-tube babies and donor artificial insemination can help couples who are unable to have children through the usual means. Embryo transfer might be a boon to a woman who, though fertile, is unable to carry her baby to term, and miscarries. Another woman might wish to have a natural child, but not wish to go through the nine months of pregnancy because it might interrupt her career. A dying woman who is pregnant might have her child born by having the embryo transferred to a healthy woman. Or, a lesbian who wishes to avoid male sexual contact but wants to raise a child of her own might opt to be artificially inseminated. And these procedures have obvious value in animal breeding — fertilized eggs from prize animals, for instance, may be frozen for use years after the death of pedigreed parents.

But with the pluses, there are the minuses, and there are plenty of those.

Take donor artificial insemination, a technique that has

been used to conceive humans since the late 1800s and that produces some twenty thousand babies every year. For one thing, long-term storage of sperm — in vats of liquid nitrogen at a temperature of 321 degrees Fahrenheit below zero — could cause it to lose its potency or alter its genetic blueprint. Some years ago, the Council on Population of the American Public Health Association pointed out that although many healthy children have been born from sperm frozen for ten years, there is no guarantee that such sperm will always produce offspring.

There is the possibility of misuse. If, for instance, only the sperm from selected donors were accepted, a master race might be created. Given individual biases about race and personality traits, one has to ask the question, Who makes the choice and what mold does he or she choose? Scientists can already increase the odds of a boy or a girl being born by sperm-screening and sperm-treatment techniques. If one can pick the sex of a child before it is conceived, what effect would there be on a community that, say, decided it wanted a preponderance of one sex over the other? Would the imbalance affect the family unit as we know it? What would it do to our ideas about parenthood?

Improving a race or a breed by selectively mating individuals with desired characteristics is known as eugenics. The English scientist Sir Francis Galton (1822–1911), a cousin of the famed naturalist Charles Darwin, believed that if society really wished to excel, then it had to cultivate only worthwhile talents and blot out the negative traits like poor health and inferior intelligence. Especially talented people, he felt, should have more children than those in ordinary occupations. His emphasis, of course, was on nature over nurture — the latter referring to the environmental factors that we know do play a part in how we develop and what we become.

A prime example of how the science of eugenics can be misused came during the rule of Adolf Hitler in Nazi Germany. In the fall of 1939, the dictator signed an order calling for the extermination of all people who were mentally defective or who had an incurable disease. By the winter of that year, several thousand people who fit that category had been led off to execution camps to be shot. Compulsory death for the useless and the undesirable, Hitler reasoned, would improve the species as well as conserve food and free necessary hospital beds. Later, the Nazi regime went so far as to kidnap young Nordic girls — blond, blue-eyed, and tall — and force them to mate with selected German soldiers. The purpose was to breed a "pure" stock that would gradually take hold and sustain an empire that was to have lasted for thousands of years.

More recently, in 1980, American newspapers headlined the disclosure, in Los Angeles, of an exclusive sperm bank that was collecting the sperm of Nobel Prize winners and offering it to carefully screened women who would bear exceptionally bright children. One of the acknowledged donors was Dr. William B. Shockley, the seventy-year-old Nobelist in physics from Stanford University who has long held that intelligence is the product of our genes, and that some races are genetically inferior to others. "I welcome this opportunity to be identified with this most important cause," said Shockley in an interview with the

Los Angeles Times. "I am endorsing the concept of in-creasing the people at the top of the population."[7]

The bank had been set up by Robert K. Graham, a seventy-year-old retired businessman who revealed that at least five Nobelists had already donated their sperm and that two dozen women had contacted his repository. Three, he added, had become pregnant.

"The principles of this may not be popular," said Graham. "But they are sound. We're trying to take advantage of the possibilities of genetics. So far, we have refused to apply to humans what we already know and apply to animals and plants."[8]

Not every scientist agreed with the concept. Said biologist Salvadore E. Luria, an MIT Nobelist: "I think it's a disgusting example of elitism. Nobody can predict everything about his inheritance." Another Nobelist, who asked to remain anonymous, commented: "I question the intelligence of the individual who believes that by doing this — and this goes for the women as well as the men — that they'll increase their chances of producing a better human race. They tend to forget that genetics is a complex science that does not work independently of environment, and that our offspring are not only the products of a mother and a father, but of generations of relatives long gone."[9]

Those who do not take the bank seriously generally agree with that statement. While individuals may inherit many traits — color and shape of eyes, hair color, size of bodies, basic mental ability, and sometimes special aptitudes such as those for music or painting or mathematics — there is little disagreement that the amount of what is learned depends also on the environment. It has been pointed out that identical twins may inherit an equal talent for music, but that the twin who studies music will be far more accomplished than the one who does not.

Scientists cannot predict with any degree of accuracy the presence of desirable traits such as intelligence and physical fitness. What they can do, however, is predict which individuals are more at risk of bearing defective children because of an inherited disease. They can also warn certain couples against mating and, in effect, aim at improving the human race by careful selection.

An exception to the generally accepted idea that characteristics acquired during a lifetime are not passed along genetically came during the 1940s in Stalin's Soviet Union. Biologist Trofim Lysenko believed and taught that acquired characteristics could be handed down — a view that appealed to the Soviet leaders, who dreamed of fashioning a new breed of citizens by social conditioning. It is a view, however, that has been generally discredited.

Opponents of eugenics also argue that the whole concept of selective breeding might backfire. As Professor James E. Bowman of the University of Chicago has expressed it, someone seeking a superior child might produce offspring with the brain of an Albert Einstein, but the morality of a Richard Nixon.

Other problems are raised by donor artificial insemination. Some people have argued that using sperm from an anonymous donor is adultery on the part of the wife, even though her husband may give his permission, and even though there is no contact between the woman and the sperm donor. There was, in fact, a case in Nice, France, in which a court granted a husband's rejection of the paternity of the child born to his wife after the procedure. She said that her husband had consented, but he later denied it. Under French law, the court could have granted his rejection of fatherhood even if it were proved that he had consented.

The question of legitimacy has been raised in this country, too. In several states, A.I.D. children are considered illegitimate, or their rights of inheritance are not clearly defined. Take the case of a woman whose husband is sterile. The couple agree that she should be artificially impregnated, and she is given sperm from an anonymous donor. The child is born, and some time later the couple divorce. Should the husband be responsible for supporting the child, just as he would if he were the natural father? A California court ruled that he must be, and so, too, have the legislatures in several other states. A few doctors, concerned about possible child-support disputes, mix the husband's sperm with that of anonymous donors to confuse the issue of who is the real father. Other physicians disapprove of this practice, saying that an A.I.D. child should be able to trace his or her genetic origin to a specific donor. This raises the issue of whether donor records should be available to scrutiny by an offspring — since donors generally request anonymity as a condition of their donating sperm — or even whether records should be kept at all.

Other problems have been raised by what has come to be known as surrogate mothering — that is, artificially inseminating another woman to bear a couple's child. In 1976, a man advertised in the newspaper for a substitute mother to have his child because his wife was unable to bear children and because he felt it was immoral for him to have sexual relations with another woman. Nearly two hundred women answered the request, each agreeing to the father's terms that he was never to meet the woman selected. When at last a woman was chosen — she was unmarried and had never had a child — a sample of the man's sperm was injected into her uterus. A baby girl was eventually born. The man's wife, who was a bit skeptical of the arrangement at first, ultimately took the baby in as her own. It cost the father ten thousand dollars — seven thousand for the surrogate mother, the rest for legal and medical fees.

In 1979, in Detroit, another couple identified only as George and Deborah paid a woman friend to bear their child after insemination with George's sperm. But a year later, also in Detroit, a judge refused to approve the plan of a childless couple to pay a woman five thousand dollars to have a baby for them. "You end up with baby-trading, money-market babies," observed Judge Roman S. Gribbs of the Wayne County Circuit Court.

These stories raise several important ethical and legal questions. There is, first of all, the propriety of advertising for a surrogate mother. Is it proper? Is hiring one's body out to bear a child, and then, in effect, selling the child, moral? Is a husband who advertises for a surrogate mother selfish and inconsiderate of his wife? Would it not be better for a childless couple to adopt? Is the child born of such an arrangement illegitimate because father and natural mother are not married?

Dr. Miriam Mazor, a psychiatrist at Boston's Beth

Israel Hospital, has said she suspects that in such matters "everything hinges on the relationship between the people involved and the prevalence of the custom." She adds that there is historical precedent for the procedure. "In the Bible, Rachel's handmaiden had her baby for her. It was okay for Rachel, but I don't know if contemporary America is ready for it." Moreover, she says, problems might arise if the woman who bears the child — the "incubator mother" — has never had a child before. "If it were her first," says Dr. Mazor, "her feelings might be different, and she might have misgivings about relinquishing it. In any event, it's all very new, very sensational. But once there's a social precedent, it may turn out to be another alternative for couples, and maybe we won't say it's a terrible thing."[10]

Says another Boston-area counselor, addressing the issue of the surrogate mother's emotions:

In a course I took at Harvard Medical School a few years ago, I suggested that there are some women who simply like the experience of being pregnant, but not necessarily the responsibility that comes with raising children. I said that some women have expressed the feeling that fulfillment, for them at least, meant being pregnant, delivering a child, but no more. I suggested that they might well serve as surrogate mothers, only I think I used an unfortunate term, like "baby banks." Well, the look on the face of the lecturer couldn't have been worse if I had spoken favorably of Hitler's breeding experiments when they had SS men impregnating women in bordellos outside of Munich. I just don't think we're ready for hiring wombs.[11]

Many of the questions that arise in connection with donor artificial insemination are also raised when discussing *in vitro* fertilization. When a woman donates an egg to be fertilized in a dish, and that egg is transferred to another woman, who is the mother? Which woman would have the right to decide to terminate the pregnancy if tests detected some abnormality in the fetus? If the woman who donated the egg died before the child was carried to term by the other woman, would the survivor become the mother automatically? Questions are also raised in connection with the laboratory process. We've already mentioned that frozen sperm as used in donor artificial insemination could be genetically damaged if kept too long in a deep freeze. The same thing could happen when egg and sperm are mingled outside the womb in a laboratory dish. Does anyone know for sure what effect this artificial environment could have on a delicate, dividing cell? What if the crucial temperature at which it must be maintained is accidentally altered just a degree or two? A power failure, for instance, could do it. What if a sudden jolt in the laboratory shakes the culture dish just enough to nudge the fragile cellular contents? Might that not result in the development of a deformed or handicapped fetus when the egg was implanted in a woman?

If such questions are difficult to answer, consider how much more complicated events might be if scientists ever carried *in vitro* fertilization to its next logical step — fashioning an artificial womb complete with amniotic fluid, to simulate that of a woman. Then, not only would the egg be removed from a woman and fertilized in a dish, but it would be carried to full term in the incubator.

Ethical, legal, and technical questions would surely swirl about such a feat.

In March of 1979, the Ethics Advisory Board of the U.S. Department of Health, Education and Welfare advised Joseph A. Califano, then secretary, that basic embryo research — including laboratory creation of embryos — was ethically acceptable under certain circumstances. The board held a dozen public hearings and concluded that although the human embryo is entitled to profound respect, "this respect does not necessarily encompass the full legal and moral rights attributed to persons."[12] Six conditions were, nevertheless, imposed on researchers:

1. Fourteen days is to be the limit for a fertilized egg to be sustained in the laboratory. This coincides with the time during which an embryo would normally complete its implantation in a mother's womb.

2. Donors of eggs and sperm are to be fully informed of the purpose of the experiment, and their consent obtained.

3. If embryo transfer is to be performed, the transfer is to be attempted only with egg and sperm from married couples.

4. If the procedure contains risks of abnormal offspring "higher than those associated with natural human reproduction" the public is to be told.

5. The research must comply with HEW regulations governing human experimentation.

6. The primary purpose of the experiments is to establish the safety and efficacy of embryo transfer, and to obtain scientific information not obtainable in any other way.

The HEW decision has touched off a debate about what the role of the federal government should be in regard to morally questionable or socially problematic research, and whether the government should continue to encourage the highly technological approach to disease and dysfunction represented by such techniques as *in vitro* fertilization.

Moreover, one has ultimately to question whether laboratory conception and birth rightly fall within medicine's boundaries at all. Dr. Leon Kass, a leading authority on ethical issues in medical research and practice, and a professor at the University of Chicago, asks these questions: "Who is the patient here? What is being treated? Is anything really being healed? Is the physician not being turned into a mere technician serving the desire of patients, notwithstanding the fact that, in many cases, these will be reasonable desires? I think everyone would acknowledge that this kind of service falls, at best, on the periphery of medicine, and some of its extensions might indeed fall on the outside."[13]

Kass has another criticism:

It does not address the questions of, for example, the causes of infertility or the possible measures to prevent tubal obstruction. Granted that one has limited federal support for research bearing on infertility, it would seem to me prudent and sensible to take a long-range view and to begin to explore questions of cause and prevention. We do know, for example, that gonorrhea and pelvic inflammatory disease are perhaps the leading causes of tubal obstruction in women — they account for probably a third of the cases. It would be curious if, with the aid of federal support, we had a program of petri-dish babies before we had a vaccine against gonococcus. That strikes me as bizarre.

With regard to whether the federal government ought to be involved, Kass observes:

It is estimated that there are approximately 500,000 married women in the United States with blocked oviducts whose only hope for having a child of their own might be through in vitro fertilization and embryo transfer. Add to this others who could use surrogate pregnancy. The number might go up still further if people continue to have tubal ligations which they then try to have reversed, unsuccessfully. It is hard at the moment to estimate the costs of a baby provided by in vitro fertilization, but a conservative figure would be $5,000–$10,000 per child. Given conservative estimates of cost and conservative estimates of numbers, we are talking about $2.5–5 billion. One could question whether it is fiscally wise for the government to embark on this program, especially if — as would seem likely — this will count as a medical service and, therefore, be included under Medicaid, national health insurance, or some other provision for payment. It is not clear that people would tolerate having something like this available only on a fee-for-service basis.

Kass regards the *in vitro* research as morally questionable, but points out that many people would view it as totally objectionable.

Many people who have gone along reluctantly with the liberalization of abortion nevertheless hold views that the human embryo is not nothing. In the absence of an over-riding concern, they would think that the embryo deserves some protection; in any case, they would be horrified by the prospect of scientists filling laboratories with human embryos for experimentation. No amount of relief of infertility, it seems to me, would be worth the further disaffection and civil contention that the lifting of this moratorium would be likely to produce. Whether I am right or the public is right on the morality of this research, the public's view is a matter of great concern, and I think our policy makers disregard it at their peril.[14]

Nuclear Energy and Nuclear Waste

In the damp dawn of July 16, 1945, near Alamogordo, New Mexico, scientists exploded the world's first atomic bomb in a test that ushered in a new age. The force of that blast was equal to that of nineteen thousand tons of TNT.

"We did the devil's work," J. Robert Oppenheimer, one of the scientists responsible for the bomb's creation, said later.

A few weeks after the test, on August 6, an American B-29 bomber flew over enemy Japan and dropped an A-bomb nicknamed Little Boy on the city of Hiroshima, setting off an explosion that left some ninety-two thousand persons dead or missing. Three days afterward, another bomb, named Fat Man, was dropped on Nagasaki, leaving forty thousand dead or missing. Thousands of others have died over the years from the aftereffects of radiation.

Each of these awesome weapons produced as much energy as would setting off a stack of explosives the size of the Washington Monument, and the realization that just one plane could deliver such destruction brought World War II to a speedy end with the surrender of Japan.

Proponents of the Bomb, then as now, have argued that dropping the two bombs was correct because those acts ended what had all the earmarks of being a much longer war with heavy casualties on the American side. "Nobody is more disturbed over the use of the Atomic bomb than I am," said President Harry Truman, who made the decision to use the weapon and who never showed any remorse over it. "But I was greatly disturbed over the unwarranted attack by the Japanese on Pearl Harbor and their murder of our prisoners of war. The only language they seem to understand is the one we have been using to bombard them. When you have to deal with a beast you have to treat him as a beast. It is most regrettable but nevertheless true." Later, Truman remarked, "It occurred to me that a quarter of a million of the flower of our young manhood were worth a couple of Japanese cities, and I still think they were and are."[15]

Opponents argue that the bombs should not have been used as they were against civilian populations; that the scientists themselves should not have worked on such a project or should have, at least, protested; and that merely setting off a well-publicized blast would have been enough to deter the enemy, who could not have mistaken its potential for mass destruction.

Today, as more destructive nuclear weapons are produced by the superpowers and more nations acquire a nuclear capability to build up their national prestige, the arguments have intensified. Those who wish to maintain an adequate, if not superior, defensive and offensive posture, say the proponents, must build up their nuclear arsenal or face subjugation or total annihilation at the hands of an enemy. Those who feel the risks are too great call for a ban of all such weapons, or for at least a halt to their spread and further development. Among those calling for a ban are the Physicians for Social Responsibility, a group who argue that there can be no winners in a nuclear war since worldwide fallout would contaminate the globe for generations, atmospheric effects would severely damage all living things, and recovery would be impossible because the economic, ecologic, and social fabric on which all human life depends would be destroyed.

Even as far back as September of 1945, a month after the first atomic bomb was dropped on Japan, scientists were expressing concern over what they had wrought. At Los Alamos, New Mexico, where the bombs were fashioned, the scientists who had worked on the weapons prepared a statement, which they transmitted to the Interim Committee of the Secretary of War. "In the years of unrelenting wartime emergency," they said,

> we, a group of scientists, worked on the development of the atomic bomb. We were aware of the fact that our labors were directed to an end which was certain of realization in the not too distant future. We worked in

the fear that our enemies might be first to create the atomic bomb and then would use it to subjugate the world. From the beginning, we were aware that the scientific and military success of our work would bring both new dangers and new possibilities of human benefit to the world. Until recently, our work was clothed in secrecy. Now that success is achieved and the nature of our work is no longer secret, we believe that we should speak publicly of the profound consequences of this development. If these consequences are to be for the better, if disasters are to be avoided, it is necessary that every citizen come to appreciate the potentialities of our new mastery over nature. Only through such understanding can we hope that our democracy will be able to make wise use of the recent discoveries.[16]

More often than not, one's political beliefs color which view is held. Thus, we hear of right-wing "hawks" who favor the Bomb opposing left-wing "doves" who are against it. The problem with these labels is that they lead us to believe that devils are pitted against angels — which is by no means always the case. It is important to realize that not everyone who lines up with pro-nuclear forces is a trigger-happy warmonger or, in the case of nuclear power plants, turns a deaf ear to the possible adverse effects of a nuclear accident. Nor is every "dove" a weak-kneed defeatist who is willing to sell his or her country out as the price of "No More Nukes."

The decision to be pro- or antinuclear is not an easy one to make, nor is it necessarily a question of right versus wrong. Atomic energy is not an evil in itself, no more than is electricity or alcohol, sex or gambling. All of these can be subverted, of course, and can do immense harm, but the question one has to ask when discussing nuclear power is why we need or want to harness such a terrible force, and if it's worth the risk. Are nuclear weapons like the hydrogen bomb, a device of such colossal force that it employs an atomic bomb as a trigger, to be used to defend ourselves or to subjugate other nations? What choice do we have if other nations have nuclear capability and refuse to give it up? Wouldn't it be better to have no nuclear forces — a situation that might mean living in peace under the rule of some stronger military nation rather than risking the chance of being obliterated? Is a nuclear arms race really a safe way to preserve the peace?

What would be the effect of an intensified peacetime nuclear weapons race on the development of other nuclear technology that might better serve the public? Wouldn't it use up money and talent needed for peacetime applications? And what of nonmilitary uses of nuclear energy? Are our resources of other fuels so imperiled that we must continue building nuclear power plants if we are to survive as a nation? Wouldn't building all these plants with the radioactive gases they emit contribute to the total radiation dose each of us receives, and thus injure our health and possibly that of our offspring through genetic damage?

In this controversy, one must separate nuclear weaponry from nuclear power plants. While both employ the energy of the atom, and both pose hazards to life and health, they are built for very different purposes — purposes that must be weighed independently of one another. Nuclear power plants are not atomic or hydrogen bombs designed to kill hundreds of thousands of people, and if we decide to oppose nuclear missiles and the buildup of an arsenal on moral grounds, it should not automatically follow that we are opposed to the construction of a power plant in a given area. Many scientists, in fact, oppose the nuclear arms race but are strongly in favor of nuclear energy for industry, provided it is made as safe as humanly possible. The risks and the benefits are different in each of these two uses of atomic power, and to make a doctrinaire decision when considering them is akin to opposing abortion because you oppose capital punishment — something that, in the interest of consistency of views about the sanctity of human life, seems logical but rarely happens.

The potential dangers are not to be taken lightly. Scientists know, for example, that high-level radiation exposure can increase the risk of contracting leukemia and thyroid cancer, can cause premature aging of the skin, and chromosome damage, which results in the loss of important genes. With the agents of heredity thus altered, abnormal offspring can be born. Radiation at low levels — the sort of radiation to which we are exposed from, say, medical x-rays or television sets — also can damage living tissues, although there is disagreement over how serious such damage is. Some scientists claim that the risks of low-level radiation have been underestimated, and that low dose rates are not as safe as supposed. Fallout, the debris that results from nuclear weapons tests, and radioactive contamination of the soil are also health hazards. Strontium 90 is one component of fallout. A radioactive isotope created by atomic fission — the release of energy by splitting atoms — it is similar to calcium, and is taken up by plants and animals. When it gets into the body through contaminated food, it is deposited in new bone material, and its radioactive properties can destroy the bone marrow cells that manufacture red blood cells. Severe anemia or leukemia may result.

As a consequence of the accident at Three Mile Island, in which large amounts of radioactive products were released into the reactor cooling system and containment building, increasing attention has been focused on the effects of such an incident on the physical health and psychological well-being of people living in the vicinity. Moreover, industry is changing the design and operation of the nuclear plants in an effort to make them safer. Opposition to plant construction — at this writing, seventy-two are in operation in the United States and ninety are under construction — has been vocal and sometimes violent. At Seabrook, New Hampshire, to cite one example, alliances of antinuclear groups have picketed, attempted to tear down fences around a nuclear plant site and halt construction, clashed with police, and been arrested *en masse.*

The protests and the picketing still go on in various parts of the nation, and not without good reason. Here is how authors Richard Curtis and Elizabeth Hogan have defined the problem:

> Each [power] plant will be fueled with a great many times the amount of uranium required to destroy Hiroshima. Under certain circumstances a portion of the intensely radioactive contents of such a reactor can be

released into our environment in the form of gas or finely divided particles. This material has been characterized as a million to a billion times more toxic than any known industrial agent, and under not unusual weather conditions could fall out over a large area. Under less common but still conceivable conditions it could blanket a territory as large as one twentieth of the continental United States.

Despite the fact that atomic power and reactor technologies are still saturated with unknowns, these reactors are going up in close proximity to heavy population concentrations. Some have even been proposed for location in the heart of a city. Most will be of a size never before attempted by scientists and engineers; they are, in effect, experiments.[17]

Apart from the possibility of another accident like what happened at Three Mile Island, there is the very serious problem of radioactive wastes, the unavoidable result of producing nuclear weapons and electricity from reactors. Called the power industry's Achilles' heel, these wastes fall into different categories. There is high-level waste, generated when spent fuel is reprocessed to salvage usable elements, or present in discarded fuel assemblies; low-level waste, such as contaminated protective work clothing, tools, cleanup solutions, and discarded medical and lab items; and uranium tailings, the fine residue from mining and milling operations.

What to do with these waste products — which can remain hazardous for hundreds or thousands of years depending on the components — is the crucial issue. "For more than thirty years," said President Carter, "radioactive wastes have been generated by programs for national defense, by the commercial nuclear power program, and by a variety of medical, industrial and research activities. Yet past governmental efforts to manage radioactive wastes have not been technically adequate. Moreover, they have failed to involve successfully the states, local governments, and the public in policy and program decisions."

The waste buildup has been enormous. As of 1979, some 75 million gallons of highly radioactive liquid wastes and 5,900 metric tons of used nuclear reactor fuel had been generated. Add to all that 140 million tons of radioactive tailings and 66 million cubic feet of contaminated gloves, tools, and the like, and it is no wonder that antinuclear forces are as angry as they are. Granted, some of the waste products are not as dangerous as others, but the fact remains that as more and more plants are built, as nuclear weapons programs continue unabated, hazardous wastes will continue to accumulate. In fact, says a report in *Amicus*, the journal of the Natural Resources Defense Council (NRDC), the current inventory of nuclear waste material is expected to double within three to four years, and the inventory produced by commercial reactors by the end of the century may be ten to twenty times as great as that currently on hand.

"The most important and immediate issue," said Dr. Terry Lash, a California molecular biologist on the staff of NRDC, "is whether the generation of large quantities of additional high level radioactive wastes should be permitted to continue unabated in light of the extended period that will be necessary to develop a satisfactory disposal facility."

Dr. Lash outlined the current status of major waste management sites, singling out Hanford Reservation in the central section of Washington State, the country's largest storage facility. High-level wastes have been stored in Hanford as alkaline liquid solutions in carbon steel tanks, some with only single steel walls. The tanks have been leaking. Approximately 500,000 gallons of high-level radioactive wastes have seeped into the Hanford soil and permanently contaminated it. And the radioactivity will probably have to be monitored as long as the area is inhabited.[18]

The leakage of radioactive wastes from holding tanks and burial sites, and the dispersal of uranium tailings by wind and water, has worried many scientists and public-health officials who are concerned over possible environmental and health effects. These authorities believe that there is *no* level below which radiation has no cancer-causing effects — that is, it may all be dangerous — and that a dose of only thirty to sixty roentgens is enough to bring about mutations. (Radiation is measured in units known as roentgens. A dose of five hundred can kill 50 percent of the time, and a dose of one thousand, which struck those who died at Hiroshima and Nagasaki, will kill immediately.)

An accident that occurred in a Rhode Island industrial plant in 1964 illustrates the hazards of working with nuclear materials and the rapidity of their effects. A worker was pouring a "dirty" mixture of uranium 235 from a cylinder into a tank containing sodium carbonate. Suddenly, what scientists call a "nuclear excursion" occurred. There was a flash of light, and the workman was hurled backward and stunned. He did not lose consciousness, and immediately ran from the building to an emergency shack, discarding his clothing as he ran. There he was joined by four other occupants of the plant who had been alerted by the radiation alarm system. Almost at once, the stricken worker complained of abdominal cramps and headache, and he began to vomit.

He was wrapped in a warm blanket, taken to a nearby hospital, then to another. Forty-nine hours later, he was dead — after having received ten to twenty times a lethal radiation exposure.

"He probably received the heaviest radiation dose of any victim of a nuclear accident," said the medical report of the mishap, "and this was the first fatality in private industry."

There have been other accidents involving human lives. The U.S. government has settled a number of claims, and has others pending, for radiation disability suffered by veterans who were exposed to atomic testing in Nevada between 1951 and 1962. These claims have been for effects that are well known — leukemia and other forms of cancer. Several others involving damage to veterans' offspring are also being considered.

An especially chilling case is one that the writer learned about while researching this book. It is an example, not only of the possible health effects of radiation, but of how those who fabricated the first atomic bombs were forced to take chances with individual lives — to sacrifice them, in effect — in order to accomplish the larger goal, the end of World War II.

The story involves Ted Lombard, a retired Boston bank vice-president who, while an enlisted man in the army, worked for two years in the processing plants of Los Alamos, pouring lead shields that would protect the scientists building the A-bombs, and fabricating metals. Twice a week, he also drove loads of radioactive materials — uranium ingots and plutonium — from Salt Lake City to Los Alamos, which was located on top of a mesa behind barbed-wire barricades and guarded by shotgun-wielding military policemen. The "hot" materials were transported in army ambulances so as not to arouse the suspicion of civilians in the area.

"I got on the hot runs — they called 'em security runs — and the only thing they told me was that if we were going out unloaded to Salt Lake and we got into an accident, they'd come get us," Lombard recalls.

> But, they said, if while we were coming back to Los Alamos with hot stuff in the ambulances, and we got into an accident or got pinned underneath, then no one was to try to help until they got a decontamination squad out there, and that could have been a long time since the furthest point was over six hundred miles away.
>
> When we finished a run into Los Alamos, we'd go to the vault, a cement building with a slant roof and a little cupola above, with no fan and a single light bulb coming down on a piece of wire.
>
> The uranium ingots we carried in bare-handed. The

plutonium was encased in lead and platinum. There was no protective clothing given us, and nobody said anything to us, never.

The only thing they did tell us was that we might be sterile for a while.

Inside Los Alamos, secrecy was so tight that Lombard and the other foundry workers were never told what they were helping to make. "Little by little, though, you get hold of things," he said.

They'd talk about hot buildings, and hotter buildings, and we'd be pouring lead shields and making lead bricks, but you know, I wasn't a physicist or anything like that and let's face it, plutonium was a newly discovered element, so who could figure it all out?

The bad thing was that we were working in what they called Sigma, or D-Building, where the final smelting and refining of the plutonium and uranium for the bomb was done. The only protective gear I had there was scuffies to wear on my feet, and we'd just throw them in a bucket when we got through. There were fumes in the air, and there was constant ingestion of that stuff, and there were no signs, no warning posted, and we were not told to take any precautions.

There were coffee urns in the hot shops and sometimes I'd go in and just sit around with the boys. You'd rinse the cups right in there, and make the coffee, with all these churnings from the machined radioactive material all over the floor, and you'd get 'em in your shoes.

There were no respirators, no ventilation system, and all you could do in hot weather was open a window.

Today, at sixty, Lombard feels that he is paying a terrible price for his involvement in the project. His hands are cracked and reddened, his skin is blotched and prematurely aged, and his teeth have crumbled at the gum line. He has fibrosis of the lungs — a condition in which the lungs' normal components have been replaced by fibrous tissue — and only 25 percent of his respiratory capacity left. He has stomach ulcers, and bleeding under the skin.

But there is further evidence of the legacy of the super-bombs in his life. One daughter, in her early thirties, is a paraplegic; lacks certain antibodies, which makes her susceptible to a host of diseases; has problems with her vision; and suffers periodic seizures. Another daughter is beginning to show some muscular difficulty, and so, too, are her two children. A twenty-one-year-old son is a deaf-mute, retarded, and subject to seizures. Another son is dyslexic — dyslexia is an inability to read understandably — and has respiratory difficulties, severe migraine headaches, seizures, and a form of diabetes.

If that medical litany were not enough to make one consider a cause-effect radiation relationship — there is no question that if reproductive cells are damaged by radiation, a mutation can be caused that will be passed on through generations — there is Lombard's eldest son. At this writing he is thirty-eight years old. He was conceived *before* Lombard entered the service — and he is perfectly healthy, proof for Lombard and several physicians that it was what happened at Los Alamos that started the biological chain reaction in his then unborn children.

The story doesn't end there. Lombard has been seeking

compensation from the government for the radiation damages he believes he and his children have sustained. But the Veterans Administration has turned down his claim, arguing that high radiation levels were not documented on his records — in the interest of secrecy, all radiation-exposure records of personnel like Lombard were destroyed — and that the term "radiation sickness" is too broad and cannot cover every illness that may occur in the future in a person who has been exposed. The VA also noted that there is no provision in the law for compensation to children whose birth defects are allegedly caused by genetic injury to the parent-veteran.

The difficulty Lombard and others like him face is proving that an unknown level of radiation exposure caused his problems and those of his offspring many years later. But as he puts it: "I'm sure there's a cause-effect relationship at work here. When you get me, and four out of four [children] with problems, some very similar, there's no question in my mind. The thing is they have definitely and deliberately submerged this whole business. They've spent all kinds of money to research Hiroshima and Nagasaki, but they haven't done a damn thing for those of us who worked on the project before they dropped the bomb."[19]

The Lombard case should make us wonder about what must often be done in the name of national security, and, as utilitarians phrase it, to achieve the greatest good for the greatest number. Do you think that the scientist in charge at Los Alamos should have informed the workers more fully about what it was they were doing? Should they have been told of the risks versus the benefits? Although Ted Lombard left Los Alamos and was able to work until his retirement, at least two others at the bomb factory did not fare as well. The first fatal nuclear "excursions" occurred there in 1945 and 1946. One of the victims died nine days after exposure, the other twenty-four days later. Is it enough for the government, which built the bomb with taxpayers' money, to say, in effect, "We're sorry, but there's not much we can do about it under the circumstances"?

Should personal health records be destroyed because of security precautions? Is destroying the records at Los Alamos any different from destroying the genetic records of an adopted child who might one day want to learn who his parents were? Or destroying the records of a patient who was injured on an operating table in order to protect the doctor who bungled the surgery? And what about responsibility? Who was responsible for what happened at Los Alamos, not only to the victims at Hiroshima and Nagasaki, but to people like Lombard? President Truman? The scientists? The government? If the government refuses to pay multimillion-dollar claims to veterans who may have been radiation damaged, declining to do so because the total cost would strain the national budget, is that a valid argument?

Consider the other side for a moment, the views of those who favor the use of nuclear energy for peaceful purposes. In countering the criticisms of nuclear energy, they maintain that solar power, conservation, wind and tidal power are valuable alternatives, but can never equal what can be done with nuclear power. Proponents believe, as do opponents of nuclear power, that America must reduce its dependence on foreign oil, but they feel that the benefits of making full use of our nuclear capability far outweigh the risks and disadvantages.

In general, the argument in favor of nuclear energy draws on the following information:

Each of us is exposed to natural radiation every day of our lives. Radiation streams down from the sun and from outer space, and is released by uranium and radium as those elements disintegrate in the earth itself. A brick house emits radiation, and so, too, does a wooden one. There is radiation in the food we eat, in the water we drink, and in the air we breathe. Our bodies themselves are radioactive.

All of this is called background radiation, as opposed to radiation that is created by scientists, and the amount that we receive often depends on where we live. For instance, someone living in Denver, Colorado, one mile above sea level, is exposed to twice as much radiation as someone living, say, in Boston.

More than half the radiation we receive is background radiation, and the rest is made by human beings. And most of the radiation that we create is given back to us, not in fallout from nuclear tests or from power plants or from nuclear waste, but in medical applications such as x-rays and radiation therapy for cancer. The power industry thus is a very minor contributor to our total radiation dose.

To understand the dosages better, we can use a simplified term, "unit." One chest x-ray may be expressed, for example, as equal to twenty units. A brick house exposes us to fifty to one hundred units a year, cosmic rays to about forty-five units, water and food to about twenty-five, soil to about fifteen. Living in the vicinity of a nuclear power plant, according to proponents of nuclear energy, exposes an individual to about one additional unit a year. Nuclear waste, moreover, it is argued, will add only tiny amounts to the environment — provided it is properly handled.

The point that is made is that radiation is a fact of life, unavoidable, and that barring accidents, spills, or nuclear war, the problem is not as alarming as opponents would have us believe.

Proponents of nuclear power generally agree that insofar as the health hazards are concerned, the incidence of diseases such as cancer — while they can, of course, be caused by radiation — is proportionately lower at low doses of radiation than at high doses. "As in the case of coffee, brandy, or medicine," says a fact sheet from the International Atomic Energy Agency, "the possible effects can be best evaluated when the quantity of radiation, the rate at which it is received and the manner in which it was received are known. For example, a single glass of whisky can be drunk and no significant side effects experienced. But what effect would drinking ten glasses have? Among other things, one would need to know whether they were drunk over 20 minutes or 20 days. . . . Radiation at low doses results in some damage to living tissues. However, the body does have mechanisms to repair this type of damage thus providing a certain level of protection against such radiation effects."

Others have analyzed the problem of spent fuel discharged from nuclear power plants, and concluded that such refuse might result in as many as seventy-four fatalities due to radiation in the next thirteen million years. That risk, said the Atomic Industrial Forum (AIF) in a position statement filed with the Nuclear Regulatory Commission, may be compared with a theoretical total of twenty-six to forty-seven billion deaths — in the same thirteen million years — just from the effects of natural background radiation. Moreover, if coal were used to replace this nuclear capacity, says the AIF, some 250,000 deaths could result from coal-generated wastes and effluents by the year 2040.[20]

Put another way, nuclear spent fuel represents the risk of a reduction in the life expectancy of about ten minutes for the average American. This is comparable to the risk that an overweight person takes by eating one extra slice of bread during his or her life, or a person takes by smoking one cigarette in a lifetime, or a pedestrian takes by crossing one extra street every three years.

Medical radiation experts have also expressed concern that the public fear, political manipulation, and confusion over nuclear waste disposal may cause a major setback for a vital segment of medicine. According to one specialist, Dr. Frederick Bonte, dean of Southwestern Medical School in Dallas, the closing of low-level nuclear disposal sites in particular is unnecessary and a threat to modern medicine, which uses radioactive chemicals and special detection devices to determine, for instance, the location of cancers and other abnormal conditions undetectable by other methods.

"I can understand the concern over burial of fuel rods from a reactor, a high-grade hazard," says Bonte. "I can understand concern of disposal of waste from a reactor that produces plutonium for weapons. That's highly lethal stuff. But in nuclear medicine we're not talking about a radiation hazard or biologically devastating material. We're talking about mildly radioactive refuse from research and everyday medical practice. And if there is no way of disposing of this material, research and medical management will be seriously impaired and for no good reason."[21]

Bonte refers to the current trend in public and political circles of condemning disposal sites of low-level radioactive waste. Such sites in Nevada and Washington State have come to national attention because of their supposed threat to humans and the environment. Sites in both locations were closed recently by the governors of those states, leaving only South Carolina as the disposal area for all low-level waste. Three sites there are now open but subject to shutdown at any time. To complicate matters, storage capacities are limited and more red tape has been added to the disposal process.

"I think the word itself — RADIATION — scares many people," says Dr. Ed Griffin, radiation safety officer for Southwestern Medical School. "They associate the word with images from Hiroshima or Army file films of nuclear explosion tests. But it's unfair to condemn, in one breath, all the nuclear sciences. What the physician and medical scientist uses is thousands, millions, even billions times less radioactive. There is a very big difference."[22]

In nuclear medicine, slightly radioactive elements suspended in liquid solution are admitted to the bloodstream. Using clever techniques, practically any organ or region of the body can be made to selectively "accept" the solution, paving the way for accurate detection by sensitive equipment. Cancer cells, for example, would then appear different from normal tissue. The extent and exact location of some tumors can be determined using these methods.

Obviously, if the solutions were not of very low radioactivity, they would be harmful to other areas of the body only inches away from the target site. This is important to remember in a discussion about the safety of nuclear medicine: most of the elements, although technically radioactive, have an effective range of only inches, and the energy emitted is slight at most. In addition, and perhaps most important to the issue of disposal, the elements typically have very fast rates of decay, or short "half-lives." In most cases the elements become completely harmless in a few days. More controversial uses of nuclear energy — power plants, weaponry, and commercial applications — employ radioactive elements that may be harmful for thousands of years and that therefore must be handled differently.

As director of radiation safety for the whole health-science center and Parkland Memorial Hospital, one of Griffin's responsibilities is to assure the safe handling and disposal of radioactive waste — the "leftovers" of medical treatment, tests, and research. "We go way beyond the federally established regulations for disposal of waste materials," says Griffin. "When you consider that federal regulations are already very safe and strict, and that our waste is typically a hundred or thousand times less than specified, you can be certain the risk to man and environment from the medical community is practically non-existent."

Dean Bonte says the disposal sites must remain in operation if medicine is to move ahead or even stay where it is. "These diagnostic techniques are too important in everyday health care to be lost in the shuffle and scare over imagined dangers."[23]

And so the matter remains, still raising questions that probably will never be answered to everyone's satisfaction. Earlier, we asked some questions about nuclear energy. Let's ask them again, along with a few others. Should the bumper-sticker expression "No More Nukes" be applied across the board to nuclear power plants, dental and medical x-rays, and industrial uses of atomic energy? If, as the Atomic Industrial Forum puts it, only seventy-four fatalities would be due to radiation from spent fuel over the next thirteen million years, shouldn't that put our minds at ease? How do you feel about the word *only* when it is used in sentences like, "*Only* one person was killed in the explosion," or, "*Only* four patients out of five hundred suffered severe effects from a new drug that may cure cancer"? If the health threat from low-level nuclear radiation is less than what a lot of people believe it to be, shouldn't we continue our uses of such radiation?

How would you feel about a nuclear plant in your neighborhood? A waste-disposal site? If you live in a brick house, would you move out to escape receiving up to a hundred units of radiation a year — about five times the dose you'd get from diagnostic x-rays in a year? Since we live in a delicately balanced environment, and because the radioactive wastes we dispose of last a long time, shouldn't we stop adding to the pool while we can in order to protect future generations? If, as one report has it, the plutonium 239 contained in the radioactive spent fuel discharged by one reactor after one year of operation would be enough to cause fatal lung cancers in the entire population of the United States if dispersed as fine particles and inhaled, is this enough to make us stop? Or do you think we ought to live out our own lives, not worry about an improbable "if," and let future generations come up with better ways of handling these problems of disposal and energy use?

Even though nuclear-power accidents are not common occurrences, is the possibility of just one happening enough to make us think twice about building more plants? It goes without saying that nuclear plants and weapons makers rarely publicize their mistakes since they don't want to alarm the public. Do you think they should let the public know every time they err, even if the goof is a minor one? Would you be more concerned if you found out that an error in a nuclear plant was caused by the men and women who work there rather than by equipment failures? Rather than going ahead with new plants, shouldn't we put the money and effort into solving the waste-disposal problem first? Should we just forget that we have plenty of uranium and scientific expertise and put enormous amounts of money into crash programs aimed at finding alternative, safer, sources of energy?

In the last analysis, one must consider the words of President Carter: "The waste generated by nuclear power must be managed so as to protect current and future generations."

And the comment of the Union of Concerned Scientists:

> This must be the foremost criterion of any waste management program. This is the minimum demanded by society. Yet, it is clear that we cannot give a total guarantee that a waste repository will never be breached or that no person or persons of future generations will ever be harmed. Requirements to this end would block necessary moves and hinder needed progress because they are unrealistic and unachievable in the real world. What society can, and should, insist on is that the risks, which we believe can be made sufficiently small and can be bounded (so that, at worst, very few people would be hurt), are made very small. Given adequate time and sufficient funds to sustain a competent program, we believe that this goal can be accomplished to the satisfaction of the bulk of technically competent observers and critics and, most importantly, to the public at large.[24]

[6]

The Press

——•◆•——

Iₙ 1973, the Society of Professional Journalists, Sigma Delta Chi, adopted a code of ethics based on the belief that the duty of members of the press is to serve the truth. "We believe the agencies of mass communication are carriers of public discussion and information, acting on their Constitutional mandate and freedom to learn and report the facts," the society wrote in the code's preamble. "We believe in public enlightenment as the forerunner of justice, and in our Constitutional role to seek the truth as part of the public's right to know the truth. We believe those responsibilities carry obligations that require journalists to perform with intelligence, objectivity, accuracy and fairness."

Freedom of the press is one of our inalienable rights as a free society, and it carries with it the freedom and responsibility to discuss, question, and challenge actions and utterances of our government and of our public and private institutions. It is, therefore, the duty of a journalist in a free society to seek news that serves the public interest, despite the obstacles.

Most of us, I think, would agree with such sentiments. But it is one thing, as we have said throughout this book, to agree with standards of any kind, and quite another to put them into practice. This difficulty is nowhere more evident than in the daily activities of the working journalist.

The journalist lives in a deadline-ridden world, a place where history is recorded in an instant, as accurately and as objectively as possible. But, unfortunately, the demands of deadlines and the individual biases and moral codes of individual writers often get in the way of desirable standards of performance. Opinions do creep into objective news stories where there should be none, if only because objectivity is not all that easy to achieve in view of the fact that a human being is behind the structure of the story. Inaccuracies do riddle some accounts of an event, or turn up in a misquote. The inaccuracies can happen because of the competitive nature of the business of disseminating news, the speed at which it is transmitted, or simply because the reporter is lazy and has not checked his or her facts thoroughly.

None of these transgressions does much to enhance a reporter's credibility. The journalist who sends the story fast in the hope of sending it first, as a posted warning in one newspaper office put it, usually ends up sending a correction. And so, too, must the reporter who follows another, less wise, dictum: "Never let the facts clutter up a good story."

But there are other considerations more serious than sloppy reporting, with which the journalist must wrestle as he or she tries to go about the proper and truthful broadcast of information. (A distinction must always be made, when discussing journalistic ethics, between absolute truth and journalistic truth. The latter is reasoned, probable, and usually partial, and acceptable in those cases where the journalist has not had the time to meticulously check all the facts and sources. Nonetheless, it behooves a reporter to quickly get at as much of the whole truth as possible.) These considerations revolve around what may simply be called fair play.

For example, while journalists must serve the public's right to know, they must also respect the privacy, rights, and well-being of those they write about — and the two demands are often at odds. Take the case of an individual strongly suspected by the police and neighbors of having committed a series of rapes. He has not yet been formally charged, and charging him may be difficult because of a lack of substantial evidence. Does a newspaper publish his name and address, justifying the move on the basis of the public's right to know about the threat he poses? Or say a reporter discovers that a kind and gentle man who has lived in a community for many years is accused of being a Nazi war criminal. Does the reporter identify the man in print?

There is controversy over how far a reporter should go to get a story. Is it fair play to eavesdrop? May a reporter pose as a policeman or use blackmail or steal secret government documents to obtain information?

Reporters have a rule of never violating a confidence. This means they do not publish material that has been given off-the-record. And it means that the reporter does not divulge a source of information if the source has requested that it not be revealed. But confidences are occasionally violated — as, for example, during World War II when a number of reporters published information in direct violation of military censorship and despite warnings that publication could jeopardize the nation's security. Should a reporter do such a thing? Should a journalist print off-the-record information if, after careful consideration, it can be argued that withholding it would do more harm than good? Should an investigative reporter divulge a source to keep from being jailed — a situation that would effectively prevent the reporter from uncovering further valuable information — or to assist a district attorney in obtaining indictments by identifying an important witness?

Lawyers, politicians, law-enforcement officials, even journalists themselves, disagree over such questions, and over the larger one that lies at the bottom of each — does the end justify the means?

For some, the answers are black and white and there is no in-between. Some argue that journalists should be more closely scrutinized, possibly licensed, their activities regulated by federal and state laws that spell out exactly what they can and cannot do under a wide variety of circumstances. Penalties, in the form of closure of newspapers or radio-television stations, fines, or jail terms, would be imposed for failure to uphold strict press regulations. Indeed, many countries have such rules. Some of those who favor press regulation would not go so far as would an authoritarian regime, but would like to see more laws that make it difficult for journalists to obtain and publish information.

Within recent years, the courts, in fact, have not always been kind to reporters. In 1972, for example, the U.S. Supreme Court ruled that a journalist does not have a First Amendment right to refuse to reveal confidential sources and confidential information to grand juries. Newsrooms may be searched, and reporters' notes subpoenaed. Newsmen and -women have been jailed for refusing to testify before grand juries. And in 1979, a judge in Wisconsin ordered a small magazine not to print a planned article that contained information on how to build a hydrogen bomb. The judge's reasoning was that free speech did not extend to publishing material that could touch off a nuclear holocaust.

No discussion of press freedom and the ethical dilemmas associated with that right can be complete without mentioning John Peter Zenger, a colonial printer who had come to New York from Germany. This courageous publisher of the *New York Weekly Journal* wrote barbed articles criticizing the oppressive administration of the greedy and dishonest governor, William Cosby. In 1734 Zenger was arrested and imprisoned, charged with printing stories that tended to "raise factions and tumults among the people of this province, inflaming their minds with contempt for His Majesty's government, and greatly disturbing the peace." While Zenger was in prison, the newspaper — which missed publishing one issue — printed the following notice:

To all my Subscribers and Benefactors who take my weekly Journall. Gentlemen, Ladies and Others; As you last week were Disappointed of my Journall, I think it

Incumbent upon me to publish my Apoligy which is this. On the Lords Day, the Seventeenth of this Instant I was Arrested, taken and Imprisoned in the common Gaol of this City, by virtue of a Warrant from the Governor, and the Honorable Francis Harrison, Esq and others in Council of which (God willing) Yo'l have a Coppy whereupon I was put under such Restraint that I had not the Liberty of Pen, Ink, or Paper, or to see, or speak with People, till upon my Complaint to the Honourable Chief Justice, at my appearing before him upon my *Habias Corpus* on the Wednesday following. We discountenanced that Proceeding, and therefore I have since that time the Liberty of Speaking through the Hole of the Door, to my wife and Servants by which I doubt yo'l think me sufficiently Excused for not sending my last week's Journall, and I hope for the future by the Liberty of Speaking to my servants thro' the Hole of the Door of the Prison, to entertain you with my weekly Journall as formerly. And am your obliged Humble Servant.[1]

For nine months, Zenger edited his newspaper "through the Hole of the Door" of his prison, and on August 4, 1735, he was brought to trial. His attorney was Andrew Hamilton, one of the colonies' most renowned lawyers. Hamilton delivered an eloquent and powerful defense of his client, arguing that the allegations printed in Zenger's newspaper were true, and, therefore, not libelous. "The question before the court and you gentlemen of the jury," he said, "is not of small nor private concern; it is not the cause of the poor printer, nor of New York, alone. No! It may, in its consequence, affect every freeman that lives under a British government on the main of America. It is the best cause. It is the cause of liberty . . . the Liberty both of exposing and opposing arbitrary power by speak- and writing Truth."[2]

The jury accepted Hamilton's argument, and Zenger was released, a verdict that established truth as the principal defense in American libel suits.

Truth must, of course, be the journalist's ultimate goal. But, is reporting it always justified? In a way, the question is the same as the one we asked earlier about whether a patient should always be told the truth. Reporters, who often learn many truths about a given story, must pause every so often to weigh the effects of the facts they publish — just as a doctor must determine whether telling a patient all will harm him or her.

Earlier, we posed some difficult questions about whether or not to identify a criminal suspect before he is charged, or an accused Nazi who has been living a quiet and respectable life. We said that something called fair play and the privacy and rights and well-being of those about whom the truth is told must be considered. This implies that the press also has the responsibility *not* to print a particular story because it could unjustifiably damage an individual's reputation or the nation's security. It is doubtful that many journalists are eager to destroy a person's character, or jeopardize their own country's safety, despite what some of the more vocal press critics would have us believe. The problem arises in deciding what is in the public interest — and editors have different ideas about that.

Some editors — indeed, most — believe that the information and enlightened opinion that are published should not be presented merely to satisfy a reader's morbid curiosity. Other editors don't see it exactly that way, and stories often appear that are filled with every lurid detail of a crime or an individual's private life. The latter approach defines the public interest not as the general welfare of the public, but as the public's interest *in* a subject — or what is thought to be the public's interest in it — no matter how sensational or bizarre. As the *New York Times* columnist James B. Reston put it some years ago: "My own view is that we are very good at reporting violence and the consequences of violence but not nearly as good at reporting the causes of violence. Our timing and emphasis are faulty. We are not getting to Watts and Harlem, Saigon and Santo Domingo early enough. We are there with the cops and the soldiers and the firemen right after the explosion but not doing enough about reporting on all the inflammatory social dynamite that is lying all around us before it catches fire."[3]

Although Reston's comments were written before the media's role in the celebrated Watergate affair — a role that stands as another example of the need for a free press and as evidence that the media can be issue-oriented when they have a mind to — they still have a ring of truth about them. There is no question that the press does often react to crises in predictable, sensationalized ways, or panders to lower tastes if it feels its audience will buy what reporters call "junk" stories.

Though we know that the press entertains as well as informs and educates, this doesn't mean that everything that is entertaining and true ought to be printed, or that just because a reader wants to know a certain fact he or she should get it. So, how far does one go in reporting the truth? Consider these dissimilar cases in which editors were called upon to make judgments about whether to print or not, and ask yourself what you would have done if you had been in charge of the newsrooms.

On June 13, 1971, while the United States was immersed in the Vietnam conflict, the *New York Times* began publishing the secret papers of a Pentagon study that traced the nation's growing involvement in Southeast Asia. Daniel Ellsberg, one of the men who worked on the classified study, later admitted that he was the source of the material first published in the newspaper. He did not say, however, how or when he leaked the documents to the *Times,* and about all the newspaper revealed about its role was that it obtained some seven thousand pages through the investigation of one of its Washington reporters. Eventually, other American papers obtained segments of the Pentagon Papers, and began publishing, an action that irritated the U.S. Justice Department and prompted that agency to "respectfully request" that publication be halted. The government maintained that printing top-secret documents violated the espionage laws and endangered national security. The *Times* and other newspapers "respectfully declined" the Justice Department's request to desist, on the grounds that it was in the interest of the people of the United States to be informed of the material in the documents.

The events of the next few days were a whirlwind of legal maneuvering and journalistic history-making. The Justice Department tried to get the *Times* to turn over its documents. The *Times* refused. Lower courts then temporarily halted publication of the papers. Eventually, the U.S. Supreme Court was asked by the *Times* to end restraints on its series of articles. The high court agreed to rule on the issue, and finally on June 30, the decision came. The headline in the July 1 issue of the *New York Times* told journalists what they wanted to hear: SUPREME COURT, 6–3, UPHOLDS NEWSPAPERS ON PUBLICATION OF THE PENTAGON REPORT; TIMES RESUMES ITS SERIES, HALTED 15 DAYS.

Were the *Times* and the other newspapers justified in publishing secret material? Is the Pentagon Papers case similar to and as important as the John Peter Zenger case? What of the way in which the documents were obtained? Obviously, the Pentagon did not make them public. Because they were, in effect, stolen secrets, didn't the newspapers have a responsibility — just as do any citizens who find or possess stolen property — to report immediately to law-enforcement agencies? Shouldn't the newspapers have at least gone directly to the government and asked which portions of the secret documents could be safely published? Isn't an American journalist being disloyal to his or her country by publishing detrimental material?

Some of these questions are not answered easily. Even today, long after the Supreme Court's ruling, one can find judges and government officials who believe that publication of the Pentagon Papers set a dangerous precedent that might prevent the government from protecting the security of the country in a time of future crisis.

A. M. Rosenthal, managing editor of the *New York*

Times, when asked whether it troubled him that the material he published was classified, responded:

> Obviously, you don't just blithely not consider a thing like that. However, most of us have been around a long time in the newspaper business and have covered this kind of thing. We are quite aware of classifications. We have all been involved in many stories where we were given classified material if it was information that would help the Government. We all know that very often a government classifies and declassifies not for military security reasons but for whim or political purpose. We all know that people who leave the Government write books in which they use classified information. Sometimes they get somebody to declassify it, sometimes not. We also know that none of this was current material; it concerned events only up to 1968.
>
> It just seemed to us that this information was essential to understanding the course of the war and decision-making in the U.S. Government, and we had no right not to print it. How could we say to ourselves that we have this information, which we do not consider classified, not bearing on military security; it is a treasure house of, not secrets, but insights into the process of government; and then say, sorry, we'll keep it ourselves. That is not what the American press is all about.[4]

In response to the charge that the *Times* was printing documents stolen from the government, Rosenthal replied:

> We are dealing with decisions made in government that affect the people. Can you steal a decision that was

made three years ago and that has caused consequences that a country now pays for, good or bad? How can you steal a decision like that? How can you steal the mental processes of elected officials or appointed officials? As a reporter, I was evicted from Poland. They accused me of probing into the internal affairs of the Polish government. From their point of view I was stealing their information. I never thought that Americans would buy the argument that you can steal information on public matters. As a newspaperman you are in search of as much truth as you can arrive at. Your basic philosophy in life is that, taken altogether, the truth on important matters — or as much as you can arrive at — is good. That is your occupation in life; that is your belief: that what is harmful is lack of information.[5]

With regard to the matter of disloyalty to one's own government, journalists are often torn between their professional duty to tell the truth and the traditional belief in "My country, right or wrong." Former President Harry Truman, after arguing with a group of reporters about secrecy in government, once responded angrily, "Dammit, it's your country, too, you know."

The conflict can be a difficult one to resolve. One might argue that "certain circumstances" or "being responsible" should govern whether or not a reporter prints material that could disturb the peace or create division and contempt for government, or put the nation or individuals in grave danger.

Take a most recent case involving several news organizations that knew for a number of weeks that six Americans were hiding out in Tehran while Iranian militants

were holding fifty-three other Americans hostage elsewhere in the city. The media, however, held the news of the
six's whereabouts because it was feared that publication
would endanger the lives of those in hiding and might
affect the fate of the hostages. Commented Seymour Top-
ping, managing editor of the *New York Times:*

> Cyrus Vance [the U.S. secretary of state] called me
> early one morning at home and said that the State De-
> partment felt that the substance of the story would en-
> danger the Americans and would we withhold the story.
> I told him that out of consideration for the Americans
> we would do so, but that I would expect that we would
> be told by the State Department if the circumstances
> changed so that publication would not endanger lives or
> if it appeared that the story was going to be released by
> another news organization. There was never any con-
> flict in journalistic terms. It wouldn't serve the public
> interest in any way for us to print that story and it
> would simply endanger American lives, so we were quite
> prepared in this context.[6]

It is generally agreed that the press acted responsibly
in this case and that an exception must be made on certain occasions to the rule of presenting the truth. But one
editor's idea of special circumstances that determine if a
story is to be published may not be the same as another's.
Nor are editors' perceptions of being responsible always
the same. Newspapers are, aside from their mandate to
operate freely under the First Amendment, business enter-
prises. They also exist to make money, and they are often
part of huge corporate chains. They need advertising to

survive, and the advertisers, who pay large sums of money to the papers and the radio-television industry, often express their dissatisfaction over stories that reflect badly on the advertisers' products by withholding their business.

In cases like that of the Pentagon Papers, it is fairly easy for the media to band together and view the government's heavy hand as a threat to freedom. The media also show a good deal of enterprise and aggressive reporting when the object of their wrath is a government agency, policy, or elected or appointed official.

But watchdogging the government — which is fair game and generally doesn't sue reporters for libel — is not quite the same as keeping an eye on industry and non-government employees. In the first place, the media are dealing with publicly elected officials, or appointees of publicly elected officials, and with public money. In the second, they are usually dealing with businesses and individuals who pay for the ads that keep the newspapers alive. It is no secret that some newspapers and broadcast facilities are reluctant to publicize stories that might anger an advertiser enough for it to withdraw an ad or refuse to run one.

One paper, for example, might carry details of a secret document on the grounds that to do so is in the readers' best interests — but be reticent about printing an article on the association between lung cancer and cigarette smoking because a cigarette manufacturer has said it will not run an expensive four-color ad in the same issue in which the story appears. A liquor distiller might object to articles assailing American drinking practices, an oil company might protest an anti-Arab editorial, and both might put pressure on the newspaper to desist. And, depending on the newspaper's degree of commitment to journalistic ethics, as well as its financial health, the advertiser may get what it demands. Courage is often easier for the media to express if the purse is full.

Newspapers chose to publish the Pentagon Papers despite fierce government pressure. Shouldn't they also choose to publish other information that would protect consumers from certain products — despite pressure from powerful advertisers? Isn't the public's right to know the same in both cases? Or is it? Are advertisers legitimate special circumstances, just as Americans hiding out in Iran were special circumstances? In that case, the press reasoned that publishing details of their plight might endanger their lives. Might the press not reason that if an advertiser withholds money, the paper's life might be endangered, depriving the public of a medium that it needs to be fully informed on important issues?

Newspapers also make decisions about whether to print a story or an ad on the basis of political considerations. A pro-administration newspaper might find it difficult to give prominence to stories, no matter how true, that run down the leaders of that administration. It is not uncommon for newspapers to react to an adverse report on their favorite party leader in a rival paper by assigning reporters to discredit the story. In such a case, an editor's advice might be, "Let's get another angle," a euphemism for turning up information — and it is generally factual, not fictional — that will offset the unkind article. Given the fact that there are many truths to be uncovered, and printed, is there anything especially wrong with such an approach? Isn't it a newspaper's duty to serve its readers — and if its readers happen to be people who wouldn't appreciate the adverse report, shouldn't they be given what is in their own best interests?

Then there is the matter of whether a newspaper ought to print advertisements for causes that are controversial or that run counter to the paper's editorial policy. Should a newspaper carry ads for houses of prostitution, or for the services of prostitutes? Or ads for or against abortion, the Ku Klux Klan, the American Nazi party and the American Communist party? What if your country was at war, and propagandists for the enemy wanted to advertise in your newspaper. Would you accept the ad?

Finally, with regard to this dilemma of what and whether to print, there are the Peeping Tom stories, the stories that report on the private lives of public and not-so-public people. Such stories, to use the modern vernacular, belong to what is known as gosso-journalism, the presentation of gossip that satisfies the public's curiosity — or what editors perceive as the public's curiosity. (Newspapers that don't care to admit they print gossip prefer the term "personality journalism.")

Virtually every major newspaper, and a number of national magazines, caters to this appetite for gossip, and for what one editor refers to as "Tut Tut Stories" — that is, stories at which the reader, in righteous indignation, murmurs, "Tut tut," but goes on to read and savor every word.

Gossip columnists generally confine themselves to the antics of athletes, film stars, jet-setters, rock performers,

TV personalities, and the like. Says Norma Nathan, whose column, "The Eye," appears daily on the gossip page of the *Boston Herald American:*

> Folks want to read this stuff. The public's right to know now has to include stuff like how Britt Ekland screwed up her life with Peter Sellers and the real reason Rod Stewart dropped her. I forget why. But gossip is like potato chips. You lose count after a while. But if you have one, you can't stop. . . . There suddenly seems to be an insatiable lust from readers to know everything intimate and personal about everybody. . . . It's been described as a reaction to recession, war, Watergate, Iran, a weariness with insoluble political issues. I think there is a different rationale. First, I think celebrities and people who suddenly become news are the new constants in mobile America. You can move from L.A. to Boston. But Jane Byrne is still the mayor of Chicago no matter in which town you read about her firing her photographer for taking a funny looking picture of her. Second, we're all *yentes* [Yiddish slang for a gossipy woman]. Admit it. You talk about stuff on the street. Why not read about it in the papers? Third, there is a new stress on styles. I think readers are fed up with your basic pyramid style story [a straight news story in which all the facts are presented at the outset] and they want a little action.[7]

The central issue in gossip journalism is the right of privacy, the doctrine that holds that a person has the right to stay out of the media's often harsh spotlight, to be left in peace. But newspapers, magazines, and television don't always honor that right, arguing that the public's right to know takes precedence over an individual's right to privacy. There is also disagreement over the nature of news, over who should be left alone, and over what actually constitutes invasion of privacy.

In general, when a person is part of a news story or is involved in a matter of real public interest, voluntarily or involuntarily, he or she loses the right to maintain a low profile. Thus, people whose work keeps them out front — politicians, athletes, performers, authors — are usually written about and photographed regularly with little regard given to privacy. By the same token, those who are not in the public eye have the right to keep their views to themselves, but if they agree to answer the questions of an inquiring reporter on the street, say, those opinions may be published in the newspaper. The rule of thumb seems to be that although one's personal thoughts and habits are private, the moment one goes out the front door and into the public where actions are, in effect, on display, privacy is relinquished.

"In news matter, then, invasion of privacy is encountered infrequently for the simple reason that people get into print only when they do something," one journalism professor has observed. "And what they do, usually, is news which destroys a claim to privacy. A hermit is entitled to his seclusion, but even he has no legal complaint if people think his peculiar way of life is of sufficient interest for a feature article.

"As one lawyer has said, 'A man's hope of exercising his right of privacy is to live a happy humdrum life and stay out of the way of newspapermen.' "[8]

Apropos of that lawyer's remark, consider the case of a man who, in 1910, was a child prodigy and had attracted considerable media attention. In 1937, the *New Yorker* magazine tracked him down and printed a biographical sketch that told of his rather ordinary life. The man was no longer in the news, but the magazine felt that his story was still in the public interest. Was the magazine correct in publishing the sketch? Was the former prodigy news all over again simply because a magazine determined that he was? Had his rightful privacy been invaded?

The man thought that his right to be left alone had been violated, and he sued. But he lost the case. A New York court ruled that he had not been damaged, that although he was living a private life, "his subsequent history, containing as it did the answer to the question of whether or not he had fulfilled his early promise, was still a matter of public concern. The article sketched the life of an unusual personality, and it possessed considerable popular interest."⁹

But is publication of the details of a person's past life always justified? Would you inform your readers that the popular candidate for mayor of the city, happily married and a model parent, had carried on a brief affair with a member of his staff while he was married? Is his past infidelity a matter of public concern? If you discovered that he was a recovered alcoholic, would you publish that? If you learned that a bank president had a prison record that he had hidden from everyone, would you share that fact with your readers? Would the nature of his offense be the deciding factor in printing the story?

The amount of time he spent in jail? What if you learned that your local bishop was illegitimate, a fact he kept to himself? Would you publish that? What if the bishop had fathered an illegitimate child? If you learned, on the eve of a national election, that the President of the United States, who was running for reelection, had consulted a psychiatrist prior to his taking office, would you publish such information in the paper that would be on the streets just as voters were going to the polls? Would you tell your readers that one of the community's most respectable women was once a prostitute?

Such questions are endless, and similar ones crop up every day in some newsroom. Again, circumstances are important, but in general, dredging up personal or sordid details of someone's past and printing them in a reckless manner — that is, when they have no bearing whatsoever on the story — is hardly justified in legitimate journalism. The problem, of course, is defining what is newsworthy, a difficult enough task, given the fine line between informing and entertaining.

In the last analysis, that prized quality known as good taste must enter into the decision-making process. Born of our own personal code of ethics, and hard to define, it is present when editors allow use of the words "died suddenly" in some instances of suicide, or decline to identify the victim of a rape, or to quote a public official who has made an outrageous remark in an off-guard moment.

Sometimes, the news value of a story or photograph must take precedence over good taste, or what some readers perceive as good taste. Journalists cannot and should not always grant the request of, say, a grieving parent who phones to ask that his or her son's name be kept out of a story involving a drug arrest, or a government agency asking that photographs of dead American soldiers not be published. During Franklin D. Roosevelt's years as President, the news media went out of their way not to mention the paralysis in his legs or print pictures of the apparatus he used to help him walk. One radio announcer, preparing to report on an address by Roosevelt, saw the President slip and fall in the mud on his way into the stadium, but did not mention the incident on the air; instead, he kept up a running commentary on the crowd, the weather, and the purpose of the President's speech.

Ultimately, each story decision must stand on its own, but good taste, or call it a moral sense, does have its place in journalistic truth-telling.

Thus far, we have focused on the information itself and whether or not to report it. But news is not news until it has been gathered, and one of the difficulties facing all reporters — indeed, it is often the prime difficulty — is getting the story. Knowing what news is and knowing where to get it are sometimes difficult enough, but actually obtaining the necessary information while still trying to respect the right of privacy or to stay within the law is not always easy to do.

Because information is not always handed to a reporter at a press conference or in a typewritten memo, and because many people have their own sense of what ought to be reported, a reporter must develop as many private sources of information as possible. These sources are often people who have access to material they feel ought to be released, but usually on the condition that they not be identified. The reporter goes along with this arrangement, reasoning that if he or she does not protect that person, sources of information would soon dry up because no one would be willing to go out on a limb and risk being jailed or fired when a reporter turned them in.

Developing private, personal sources of information requires that the reporter be gregarious, and that he or she become friendly with clerks and secretaries as well as with the highly placed people they work for. All of this implies, of course, that someone is giving out information that someone else doesn't want given out. Questions of ethics invariably arise. Is the secretary who, for instance, makes a copy of her boss's expense account to give to an investigative reporter acting responsibly? Is it ethical for the reporter to accept material that has been obtained by violating someone's trust? Should a reporter use information he or she has obtained with a hidden tape recorder or with an ear to someone's closed door? May a reporter pose as someone else to obtain information? Does the nature of the disguise make any difference? Or the reason for the disguise? For example, would you condone a reporter's posing as a police officer or an FBI agent to force someone to reveal information that he or she would not reveal except to a law-enforcement official? What about a reporter's posing as an orderly in a mental hospital suspected of maltreating patients? As a member of a religious sect that may be taking advantage of its members?

Should a reporter pay a bribe to obtain information?

Offer a favor? Threaten to use a negative story? Should a reporter break the law to obtain information — for instance, participate in a crime with individuals the reporter has been watching? Should a female reporter researching prostitutes pose as one, even to the point of soliciting customers and having sex with them? Should a reporter doing a series of articles on organized crime, or any illicit activity, report the details of such activities to the police before printing anything in the newspaper? After all, citizens are obligated to inform the law of illegal activities if they know of them, so why are reporters any different?

Once again, there is wide disagreement, among judges and journalists, over such questions, and simple answers are not easy to come by.

The reporter who poses as someone else to get a story is a case in point. This is by no means uncommon, and "going under," as journalists refer to the practice, has resulted in many wrongs being righted, and has often brought awards to the reporters who resorted to the tactic. Most journalists believe that an undercover operation is essential in preparing some stories, reasoning that the technique is used and accepted in all sorts of investigative work where it is known that information would never be offered or facts of wrongdoing admitted by the subject of the investigation. A report on questions of ethics in a recent issue of the *IRE Journal,* official publication of the group called Investigative Reporters and Editors, tells of one instance in which a journalist felt justified in concealing his identity.

It involved a meeting of a local of the Teamsters

Union, which had barred the press from meetings and refused to answer questions about what happens when dissidents speak up. The reporter dressed as a truck driver, went to the meeting, and took notes. "No one asked for identification, and I volunteered none," said the reporter later. And what he got was a "first-hand, eyewitness account of goons pounding the hell out of a man who tried to ask a question from the floor."[10]

Then there was the case of the Mirage Bar in Chicago, in which the *Chicago Sun-Times* bought and operated a bar where staff members filmed and taped bribes being offered and paid to city inspectors. Known as a "sting" operation, the technique is also used on occasion by law-enforcement officials trying to trap wrongdoers. "Stings" have been criticized as entrapment — luring people into compromising statements or acts that they may or may not have planned to make or do — and the *Sun-Times* was denied a Pulitzer Prize on this basis. But other journalists would have given the prize to the newspaper.

"What is entrapment?" asks Bob Greene, an investigative reporter, multiple Pulitzer Prize winner, and assistant managing editor of Long Island *Newsday*. Take the case of a paper that has a car certified as being in top mechanical shape, then has one engine wire disconnected. The car is then taken around to twenty service stations and twenty different diagnoses and prices for repair are obtained. Is that entrapment when it turns out that some of the stations were cheating and lying? Greene says no, arguing that it's legitimate, and is the only way of obtaining information about wrongdoing that might not otherwise be obtained.

"There's nothing wrong as long as you don't misrepresent yourself as someone who can compel information," says Greene.[11] That is, reporters should not try to pass themselves off as policemen, judges, or the district attorney.

Larry Jinks, editor of the *San Jose* (California) *Mercury and News*, agrees. "I think it's legitimate for a journalist to put himself in a situation to get a story that he might not be in if he were not a journalist," he says.[12]

In commenting on the Mirage Bar case, *IRE Journal*'s associate editor Dale Spencer raised the issue of a reporter who participates in a crime. "This is the area of greatest legal risk," he feels.

> The *Chicago Sun-Times* reporters who operated the Mirage Bar didn't just observe or even discuss bribes. They paid bribes. That's a crime. Other reporters in pursuit of worthwhile stories have gambled, bought drugs, done business with prostitutes. Each of those acts is a crime. Your professional duty may require you to do it; your code of ethics may justify it; but in any of those cases, you violated the law. You could go to jail. Not many reporters go to jail. The best way to avoid that is to do what the *Sun-Times* staff did: make sure some law enforcement agency knows what you are doing and why. Criminal intent is an essential element of most crimes, and by making clear your good intentions you can protect yourself.[13]

That, however, can be tricky, Spencer points out. "Suppose it is the law enforcement agency you are investigating. You can't very well announce your plans. And while you usually can find an agency you can trust to confide in, you may have some uncomfortable moments wondering how much information is being shared between agencies."

Most journalists take a situation-ethics approach in cases of the sort we've just mentioned. About the only firm rule they go by is the order from their editor, "Get the story." How far one goes in getting the story depends on how difficult the task will be.

"Sometimes the end justifies the means," says Greene, "most times it doesn't. But you can't say never. We just recognize that there are degrees in everything."

Says Jinks: "Like so much in this business, you have to make judgment calls. If you're doing something that intelligent members of the general public see as a legitimate way of getting information, then that's probably acceptable."

Freedom of the press, then, is not an absolute and hallowed right, and the journalist who takes his or her work seriously understands that. He or she knows that a reporter cannot do everything and anything to obtain a story for the simple reason that reporters are citizens too, and bound by the same laws as everyone else. The First Amendment does not permit journalists to be arrogant or dishonest or negligent of the rights of others.

As the U.S. Supreme Court has said in one of its many opinions on the First Amendment, "The newspaperman must never forget that liberty of the press is not his exclusive right but that it belongs to all people just as the other freedoms of the First Amendment. That an orderly society must impose some limits, actual or implied, on all liberties is obvious if any liberty is to be worthwhile. Absolute and total liberty results only in irresponsibility."[14]

[7]

Human Rights

—◦•◦—

Iɴ a prison, a man who has murdered his young wife and their baby is singled out by both his fellow inmates and the guards as the most despicable prisoner within the walls. He is beaten by the other men, shunned, and receives no privileges. The governor of the state has said publicly that the man will never see the light of a free day, and even the prisoner's closest relatives have denounced him. Should he be treated this way?

Consider primitive tribes living in a forest without any modern conveniences whatsoever. The men and women there have no knowledge of the outside world and its ways. A logging company discovers that the trees that surround these primitive people are prime growth, and make arrangements with the government to move the natives and resettle them elsewhere, so the lumber may be cut. Since the natives are a peaceful and simple people, and do not understand the reasons behind the move, they accept it. Does this mean that they must? Should the logging company give up its plans to cut down the trees and leave the natives where they are? Should it go ahead with its plans to move the natives, but pay them for the loss of their land, their homes, and for the unhappiness the move will cause?

Suppose a spaceship landed on earth, and its inhabitants — who looked and acted very much like humans — got out and tried to make personal contact with us. Suppose suspicious humans didn't take too kindly to this gesture and, without any attempt at communicating, shot them all down. Since murder, by definition, is a crime committed against human beings, would the killing of the aliens be murder? Although they came from another world, they were obviously intelligent beings. So wouldn't they have rights too? Should the killers be prosecuted? Would it make any difference if the aliens resembled giant insects?

We are speaking, of course, about human rights, and although it might be disputed that humanlike extraterrestrial creatures do not possess them, few would deny that they are fundamental. Our civil rights are guaranteed under the U.S. Constitution and by certain acts of Congress. Part of the Reconstruction policy of the United States after the Civil War, these amendments and acts were designed to strengthen the freedoms of recently emancipated slaves, and the term "civil rights" is most often applied today to individuals or to minority groups.

There is also a famous French document known as the Declaration of the Rights of Man, adopted in 1789, which affirmed that all citizens are born equal, are equal in the eyes of the law, have rights to liberty and property, and the right to resist tyranny. In historical importance, the document ranks with the English Bill of Rights and the American Declaration of Independence, which was adopted in 1776 and reads, in part: "We hold these truths to be self-evident; that all men are created equal; that they are endowed by their creator with certain un-alienable rights; that among these are life, liberty, and the pursuit of happiness."

Human rights are beneath the surface when we talk of slavery, racial discrimination, civil disobedience, and preferential hiring; of dissidents who are expelled from a foreign country for their unpopular views; of fetuses that are aborted; of the mentally retarded who cannot make decisions for themselves, prisoners destined for the electric chair, the subjects of human experiments, patients in hospitals, even an organized-crime figure subjected to trial by newspaper publicity. According to Freedom House, a New York–based nonpartisan human-rights organization, a staggering 1.5 billion people in 17 countries lost political rights and freedoms in 1980 — 90 percent of them in China and the Soviet Union. Some 147 million people in 15 other nations lost some freedoms.[1]

"We must now consider that natural law and the light of moral conscience within us do not prescribe merely things to be done and not to be done," said social philosopher Jacques Maritain. "They also recognize rights, in particular rights bound up with the very nature of man. The human person has rights by the very fact that he is a person, a whole who is master of himself and of his acts, and consequently not merely a means, but an end, an end which must be treated as such; the expression, 'the dignity of the human person,' means nothing if it does not signify that through natural law the human person has the right to be respected and is the subject of rights, is the possessor of rights. Some things are due to man by the very fact that he is man."[2]

Maritain points out that the philosophy of a person's rights is based on the idea of natural law, the ultimate arbiter of right and wrong; that is, as Saint Thomas Aquinas put it, "Nothing else than the rational creature's participation of the eternal law." Natural law's precepts always were and always will be, say its adherents, no matter the nation and no matter who or how powerful the one who governs. Thomas Paine (1737–1809), the English pamphleteer and political radical who came to America in 1774 and was an outspoken supporter of the American and French revolutions, would have agreed with Maritain. In his *Rights of Man,* a political work in defense of the French Revolution, he argued that civil government's existence is based on a contract with a majority of the people; its sole purpose is safeguarding the individual. Moreover, Paine preached, if a human being's natural rights are blocked by government, revolution is entirely permissible.

But although human rights and natural law may be considered fundamental and universal, we know that not everyone sees them that way. In medieval days, one spoke not of human rights but of what a man owed to his king, his church, or to the lord who owned the land he worked. Totalitarian regimes — ancient Sparta was one, along with Nazi Germany and the Soviet Union — often suppress the rights of individual citizens in an effort to bring the greatest good to the greatest number. The ends, in those nations that have gained total control over every aspect of their citizens' lives, are always seen as justifying the means.

But should the consideration of one's rights always be the governing factor in how we treat a person? Is that always possible in the real, everyday world? Aren't there times when a strong hand seems to be the only practical approach? One example might be the total control a parent holds over a child. Certainly a child's right to liberty cannot be construed to mean that the child is free to do whatever he or she pleases. Consider, also, the physician-patient relationship that respects the privacy of the patient and the confidentiality of his or her medical records. But what if the patient is a President of the United States, or a presidential candidate? Shouldn't private health records then be a matter of public record?

It is also important to differentiate, when we talk of human rights, between liberty and our "right" to such tangibles as education, health care, and a comfortable home. Merely to proclaim that we have a right to certain things does not necessarily mean that someone has a duty to provide them. Says the *Encyclopedia of Philosophy*, a definitive work on the subject:

> Human rights, in short, are statements of basic needs or interests. They are politically significant as grounds of protest and justification for reforming policies. They differ from appeals to benevolence and charity in that they invoke ideals like justice and equality. A man with a right has no reason to be grateful to benefactors; he has grounds for grievance when it is denied. The concept presupposes a standard below which it is intolerable that a human being should fall — not just in the

way that cruelty to an animal is not to be tolerated but, rather, that human deprivations affront some ideal conception of what a human life ought to be like, a conception of human excellence.[3]

Much has been made of the Soviet Union's violation of human rights, especially with regard to dissident scientists and literary figures, and the Russians' attack on Afghanistan. "When there is military aggression," said former President Carter in a message that hinted of Afghanistan to those attending a conference on human rights and peace, "there can be no human rights, human dignity or human welfare. Where there is governmental oppression, there can be no flowering of the human spirit." President Reagan, too, felt constrained to join in the criticism of Soviet morality, saying in an interview shortly after he took office that the Russians "don't believe in God or a religion, and the only morality they recognize, therefore, is what will advance the world of socialism."[4]

Reagan's comments prompted *Time* magazine to comment that harsh as the President's words may seem, they rather accurately reflect Soviet leaders' statements over the years. One example cited was a statement by Lenin, the celebrated Russian leader and Communist theorist: "We repudiate all morality that proceeds from supernatural ideas or ideas that are outside class conceptions. Morality is entirely subordinate to the interests of class war. Everything is moral that is necessary for the annihilation of the old exploiting social order and for uniting the proletariat." Another example mentioned was

Russian dictator Joseph Stalin's reply when asked by Lady Astor, first woman to sit in the British House of Commons, when he was going to stop liquidating wealthy farmers in his drive to collectivize the land. Said the Russian leader: "When it is no longer necessary."[5]

The Soviets have argued consistently that the charges of abuse have been blown out of proportion by hostile governments, that efforts by other countries to impose their own values are improper interference in Soviet internal affairs, and that under an international covenant adopted by the United Nations in 1966, they may restrict emigration, and freedom of thought, conscience, religion, expression, and association in order to protect the national security, the public order, health and morals, and the rights and freedoms of others.

Dissidents have been arrested, the Soviets have said, because they actively opposed the socialist system, often as accomplices or agents of imperialism. Finally, it is argued that the Soviet Union has never asked Western nations to change their practices as a condition of participating in U.S.-sponsored events.

In light of this, one must ask whether a nation can demand that another nation adhere to a firm code of human rights. Doesn't a country have the right to govern itself as it sees fit? Does a nation such as the United States, which was engaged for so long in a war in Vietnam — a war that was fought not because the United States was in danger but to prevent the spread of communism — have a right to criticize the invasion of Afghanistan, which took place to stifle views unpalatable to the Soviets? Was President Carter right in calling for a boycott of the

Olympics in Moscow because of the Russians' invasion of Afghanistan? What did that have to do with the attack?

Then there is the matter of civil-rights violations in this country. Do we really have a right to demand that others shape up? The Russians usually point out that their government guarantees jobs, education, health care, and housing. Virtually all over America there is evidence of slums as vile as those anywhere in the less-developed world, street violence, racial and sexual discrimination, high rates of unemployment, a health-care system that is unevenly distributed and costly. Many of our prisons remain hellholes, and the cases of exploitation and abuse of the mentally ill have been well documented, even in 1981.

It is not stretching the truth, for instance, to point out that ill-trained and overworked staff in many mental institutions resort to large doses of drugs to control and sedate patients. Some of our large corporations give lie-detector tests to employees in an effort to stop thievery; credit agencies, insurance companies, and the government invade our privacy on a regular basis; many of our citizens violently oppose the immigration of Vietnamese — people we once vowed to save from communism — Cubans and Puerto Ricans seeking better opportunities, arguing that they are taking jobs away from needy Americans. And in a Chicago suburb, recently, there was a heart-attack victim who died after police, acting on orders from the mayor, refused to allow paramedics to care for him because they were on strike.

Are we on firm ground when we criticize the way

human rights are neglected in other countries? Must we conclude that the world is a place of hard reality, that each of us does things according to a definition of right and wrong that stresses that no act is wrong if one can get away with it?

Or should we recognize that it is not important who is right — but what is right?

Finally, there is the problem of those who do not concern themselves at all, one way or the other. In a major study released in 1980, the Hastings Center in New York reported that the teaching of ethics in American higher education is frequently poor or nonexistent. Despite considerable public and academic interest in the subject, few colleges or professional schools accord it an important place. Fewer than half the schools of public policy and administration, for example, offer any course work in the subject, and only a quarter offer a significant course. If those in policymaking positions are not exposed, beforehand, to problems of deception and corruption, how, then, are they to deal with these things when they actually intrude on human rights? If professors and students resist confronting moral issues, do they have any right to complain when Big Brother watches so closely as to invade our privacy?

The protection of human rights is a basic principle of society, and a legitimate concern of all who are committed to freedom.

Afterword

—————

In 1771, Thomas Jefferson wrote a letter to a friend in which he expressed a sentiment that is understandable when one considers when in history it was written: "A lively and lasting sense of filial duty," said Jefferson, "is more effectually impressed on the mind of a son or daughter by reading King Lear, than by all the dry volumes of ethics, and divinity, that ever were written."

The ethics that Jefferson referred to, of course, was the classical conception of a subject whose primary duty was to inquire into the nature of what was good, and to formulate acceptable rules for human conduct. Ethics is still the science of right conduct and character. But where its emphasis was once solely on personal morality of the sort contained in "dry volumes," today it must focus on morality as it affects large numbers of people, even entire nations. Says Ivan Hill, president of American Viewpoint, an organization devoted to extending economic and political freedom in America by promulgating the need for honesty and individual responsibility:

Our technology has not served to make the Golden Rule obsolete, but, instead, has made its application increasingly essential. This is no Sunday School observation. In a highly complex, interdependent technological society, the tolerance for deviant behavior is narrower and shallower than in earlier times. One small bomb in a power plant can leave portions of a great city in darkness, close scores of manufacturing plants, disrupt airports, and spoil food in a hundred thousand home freezers. The few individuals who hijacked airplanes cost a vast public millions of dollars and much inconvenience. Sure, Jesse James robbed some trains in his day, but in doing so, he didn't affect the daily traveling habits of over a half million persons. The point is, as individuals and as a public, American citizens have got to be more responsible and ethical than our grandparents *needed* to be. We must understand this obligation if we hope to live in freedom.[1]

The issues that have been raised in this book are more than classroom exercises. The discussion of medical ethics, for example, may very well stimulate your moral imagination — but it may also be of some practical benefit someday when you or a member of your family is called upon to help make a life-or-death decision.

As future physicians, journalists, businessmen and -women, lawyers — indeed, in virtually every profession or occupation — you will be called upon, as never before, to consider the social and ethical implications of your work. And the decisions you make will probably have a greater impact on the general public than ever before. As a designer of automobiles, will you be motivated more by profit than by safety? As a journalist working against a deadline, will you sacrifice accuracy to beat your competition into print? As a scientist, where will you draw the line between experimenting and meddling? As a lawyer, will you be merely a "hired hand" or will you obey your own conscience and not that of your client?

Philosophy and its branch, ethics, are no longer confined to an ivory tower. Even the philosophers are aware of that. Increasingly, they are beginning to think about the very same things that you do. Philosopher Jacob Needleman of San Francisco State University has summed it up aptly:

> Traditionally, philosophy concerned itself with the fundamental questions of reality: does God exist, is there a soul, what is the relationship between mind and body, what is the good life, the difference between right and wrong?
>
> The gut-level questions that people ask themselves at three o'clock in the morning. . . . That was and still should be the role of philosophy — to help people do justice to the problems of living.[2]

Notes

1. History of Ethics

1. William K. Frankena, *Ethics* (Englewood Cliffs, N.J.: Prentice-Hall, 1963), p. 114.

2. Ibid., p. 2.

2. Medical Ethics

1. Edwin N. Foreman, quoted in *Signs and Symptoms,* Brown University, Winter 1980, pp. 3–4.

2. Ibid.

3. *Acta Apostolicae Sedis,* 1957.

4. *Society for the Right to Die Manual,* 1979–1980, p. 5.

5. B. D. Colen, *Karen Ann Quinlan: Living and Dying in the Age of Eternal Life* (New York: Nash Publishing Company, 1976).

6. John Langone, "The Life Support Dilemma," *Boston Herald American,* August 14, 1978.

7. "Withholding Medical Treatment," *Science,* August 31, 1979, p. 883.

8. "Courts, Committees and Caring," *American Medical News,* May 23, 1980.

9. Paul Langner, "She Refused Blood and Died," *Boston Globe,* September 19, 1979, p. 17.

10. Michael Conniff, "They Had to Watch Her Die," *Boston Herald American*, September 19, 1979, p. 1.

11. Quoted in Robert M. Veatch, *Case Studies in Medical Ethics* (Cambridge: Harvard University Press, 1957), p. 338.

12. In *Focus*, Harvard Medical Area, April 17, 1980, p. 1.

13. Veatch, *Case Studies in Medical Ethics*, pp. 137–139.

14. Sissela Bok, "The Ethics of Giving Placebos," *Scientific American*, vol. 231, no. 5 (November 1974), pp. 17–23

15. Ibid.

16. Ibid.

17. Joseph Fletcher, *Morals and Medicine* (Boston: Beacon Press, 1960), p. 49.

18. Melvin Levine in *Focus*, Harvard Medical Area, April 17, 1980, p. 1.

19. Veatch, *Case Studies in Medical Ethics*, p. 238.

20. Leo Alexander, "Medical Science under Dictatorship," *New England Journal of Medicine*, vol. 241 (1949), pp. 39–47.

21. Loretta McLaughlin, "Patients or Guinea Pigs," *Boston Herald*, January 16, 1966, p. 1; Henry K. Beecher in *New England Journal of Medicine*, vol. 274 (1966), pp. 1354–1360.

22. "Health and Human Rights," *World Health*, January 1976, p. 7.

23. "Most Medical Research on Convicts Called Unethical," AMA news release, July 15, 1974.

24. John Langone, "Subject of Experiments on Fetuses Aired," *Boston Herald American*, January 17, 1974, p. 18.

25. "Fetuses Essential in Research," AMA news release, September 2, 1974.

26. Langone, "Subject of Experiments on Fetuses Aired," p. 18.

27. *Omni* magazine news release, December 1979.

3. *Lawful Killing*

1. "Peace, War and Philosophy," from *The Encyclopedia of Philosophy*, vol. 5 (New York: Macmillan, 1967), p. 63.

2. Seymour M. Hersh, *My Lai 4: A Report on the Massacre and Its Aftermath* (New York: Random House, 1970), p. 82.

3. Telford Taylor, "Judging Calley Is Not Enough," *Life* magazine, April 9, 1971, p. 22.

4. "Lt. Calley and the President," *Life* magazine, April 16, 1971, p. 40.

5. Michael Novak, "The Battle Hymn of Lt. Calley and the Republic," *Commonweal*, April 30, 1971, p. 186.

6. Quoted in John Langone, *Death Is a Noun* (Boston: Little, Brown, 1972), pp. 117–118.

7. News release, Harvard University Medical Area, January 24, 1980.

4. *Ethics in Business and Government*

1. "Nixon Slide from Power: Backers Give Final Push," *New York Times*, August 12, 1974, p. 1.

2. Lynn R. Kahle in *Science News*, February 2, 1980.

3. Jeb Stuart Magruder in *Boston Globe*, June 15, 1973, p. 1.

4. William Sloane Coffin, "Not Yet a Good Man," *New York Times*, June 18, 1973.

5. Earl W. Kintner in *The Ethical Basis of Economic Freedom*, edited by Ivan Hill (Chapel Hill, N.C.: American Viewpoint, 1976), pp. 401–402.

6. Ibid., page 232.

5. Ethics in Science and Technology

1. *Chemical and Engineering News,* March 17, 1980, p. 15.

2. From the *Cancer Bulletin,* vol. 31, no. 6 (1979), Medical Arts Publishing Foundation.

3. PBC news release, undated.

4. "The Case Against Patenting Life," in the Supreme Court of the United States, October Term, 1979, no. 79–136.

5. Harold Banks, "Life Form Patent Ruling Called Serious Mistake," *Boston Herald American,* June 26, 1980, p. 46.

6. Eli Lilly news release, July 21, 1980.

7. Associated Press report by Robert Locke, March 29, 1980.

8. Ibid.

9. John Langone, "Superman Sperm Banks in Business," *Boston Herald American,* March 1, 1980, p. 1.

10. Miriam Mazor in interview with the author.

11. Interview with the author, 1979.

12. "HEW Ethics Panel Backs Test Tube Baby Research," *New York Daily News,* June 10, 1979.

13. "A Conversation with Dr. Leon Kass: The Ethical Dimensions of In Vitro Fertilization," edited transcript of discussion held November 16, 1978, at the American Enterprise Institute for Public Policy Research, Washington, D.C., p. 7.

14. Ibid.

15. Quoted by Robert J. Donovan in *Conflict and Crisis: The Presidency of Harry S. Truman* (New York: Norton, 1977), p. 97.

16. Mimeographed statement, dated September 14, 1945, distributed by W. A. Higinbotham, Building U, Room 105, Tech Area, Los Alamos.

17. Richard Curtis and Elizabeth Hogan, *Perils of the Peaceful Atom* (New York: Ballantine Books, 1970), p. xv.

18. News release, undated, from Herbert J. Farber Associates, New York.

19. John Langone, "A-Bomb Run Comes Back to Haunt Him," *Boston Herald American,* June 10, 1980, p. 1.

20. Atomic Industrial Forum, Washington, D.C., undated news release.

21. University of Texas Health Science Center, news release, December 12, 1979.

22. Ibid.

23. Ibid.

24. Ronnie D. Lipschutz, *Radioactive Waste: Politics, Technology and Risk* (Cambridge, Mass.: Ballinger Publishing Company, 1980), p. 170.

6. The Press

1. Frank Luther Mott, *American Journalism* (New York: Macmillan, 1950), pp. 33–34.

2. Ibid.

3. James B. Reston, "The Press in a Changing World," *The Quill,* June 1968.

4. "Why We Published," *Columbia Journalism Review,* September/October 1971, p. 17.

5. Ibid.

6. Dierdre Carmody, "Media Knew About Six Escapers, Didn't Tell," *New York Times* News Service, February 1, 1980.

7. Norma Nathan in address before the New England Women's Press Association, reprinted in the *Boston Herald American,* June 19, 1980, p. A19.

8. Walter A. Steigleman, *The Newspaperman and the Law* (Dubuque, Iowa: William C. Brown Company, 1950), p. 228.

9. Quoted in *The Associated Press Stylebook and Libel Manual*, 1977, p. 260.

10. "Deception by Reporters," *IRE Journal*, November/ December 1979, p. 7.

11. Ibid.

12. Ibid.

13. Ibid.

14. *Schenck v. U.S.*, 249 U.S. 47

7. *Human Rights*

1. "Repression Increased in the World in 1980," *New York Times*, January 4, 1981, p. 14.

2. *The Social and Political Philosophy of Jacques Maritain*, edited by Joseph W. Evans and Leo R. Ward (New York: Image Books, 1965), p. 49.

3. *The Encyclopedia of Philosophy*, vol. 7–8 (New York: Macmillan, 1967), p. 198.

4. "Soviet Is Mocking Reagan on Morality," *New York Times*, February 6, 1981.

5. "On Soviet Morality," *Time* magazine, February 16, 1981, p. 17.

Afterword

1. Ivan Hill in *The Ethical Basis of Economic Freedom*, edited by Ivan Hill (Chapel Hill, N.C.: American Viewpoint, 1976), p. xvi.

2. Jerry Carroll, "The Return of the Philosopher," *San Francisco Chronicle*, June 22, 1979, p. 18.

Index

to truth from physician,
46–59
Pentagon Papers, 175–176
Peoples Business Commission
(PBC), 122–125
personality journalism, 182–184
physicians
attitudes toward prolonging
life, 26–27
attitudes toward truth-telling,
47–48
and capital punishment, 95–
97
decisions in terminal cases,
20–21, 25, 32, 35
role of, 19–20
truthfulness with patients,
46–59
Physicians for Social Responsibility, 144
Pius XII, 29
placebos, ethics in use of, 53–57
Plato, 11, 12
politics
and ethics, 13, 99–108
and journalists, 181–182
privacy, right to, 169, 182–186
prolonging of life
legal issues on, 34–42
patient's rights in, 33–42
physicians' views of, 20–21,
26–27
Pseudomonas and genetic
engineering, 118
see also Chakrabarty,
Ananda

quality of life, 20–21, 64
Quinlan, Karen Ann, 36–38

radiation, 147–148, 158–159
dangers of, 151–155, 159

in nuclear medicine, 161–
162
radioactive wastes, 149–151,
159–161, 165
Reagan, Ronald, 200
recombinant DNA, 114–115,
117, 120–121
see also DNA; genetic
engineering
Reed, Walter, 66
research. *See* medical research
Reston, James B., 174
"right and wrong," 9–10, 12,
15, 16–17
rights. *See* children's rights;
human rights; patients'
rights; privacy
right to die, 31, 34–35
right to life, 31, 64
Riley, Thomas J., 92–93
Roman Catholic Church, 29,
30
Roosevelt, Franklin D., 187

Sabath, Leon D., 76
Saikewicz, Joseph, 38–40
Seabrook (N.H.) antinuclear
groups, 148
selective breeding. *See*
eugenics
selfishness, 9, 10
Shockley, William B., 132–133
situation ethics, 5
Socrates, 11, 12, 14–15
Socratic method, 6
Solzhenitsyn, Aleksandr, 97
Sophists, 11–12
Soupart, Pierre, 80
Soviet dissidents, treatment of,
97, 200–201
sperm banks, 129, 131, 132–134
Spinoza, Baruch, 13

2012